easy food for kids

easy food for kids

simple recipes for child-friendly food

RYLAND
PETERS
& SMALL

LONDON NEW YORK

Senior Designer Sonya Nathoo
Editors Céline Hughes and
Delphine Lawrance
Picture Researcher Emily Westlake
Production Controller
Maria Petalidou
Art Director Leslie Harrington
Publishing Director Alison Starling

Indexer Sandra Shotter

First published in the US in 2009
by Ryland Peters & Small
519 Broadway, 5th Floor
New York, NY 10012
www.rylandpeters.com

10 9 8 7 6 5 4 3 2

Text © Susannah Blake, Tamsin
Burnett-Hall, Linda Collister, Ross
Dobson, Silvana Franco, Liz Franklin,
Tonia George, Nicola Graimes,
Amanda Grant, Rachael Anne Hill,
Louise Pickford, Fran Warde, and
Ryland Peters & Small 2009

Design and photographs
© Ryland Peters & Small 2009

ISBN 978 1 84597 898 3

Printed in China

Library of Congress Cataloging-in-
Publication Data:

Easy food for kids : simple recipes for
child-friendly food.
    p. cm.
  Includes index.
  ISBN 978-1-84597-898-3
  1. Quick and easy cookery. 2.
Children--Nutrition.
  TX833.5.E27884 2009
  641.5'55--dc22

2009021109

Notes
• All spoon measurements are level,
unless otherwise specified.

• Ovens should be preheated to the
specified temperature. Recipes in this
book were tested using a regular oven.
If using a convection oven, follow the
manufacturer's instructions for
adjusting temperatures.

• All eggs are medium, unless
otherwise specified. Recipes containing
raw or partially cooked egg, or raw fish
or shellfish, should not be served to
the very young, very old, anyone with
a compromised immune system, or
pregnant women.

• The serving amounts given in the
recipes are approximate suggestions
only and will vary depending on
whether they are served to older
or younger children, or to adults.

contents

introduction

It can be all too easy to get stuck in a rut with the kids' dinner. When time is precious and the little ones are clamoring for some food, there is always a temptation to make that failsafe pasta dish or those favorite chicken nuggets to keep them happy with the minimum fuss. Sometimes all that's needed to bring a little variety and fun back into mealtimes is some simple inspiration. Leaf through this friendly collection of recipes and you'll find something to soothe and delight every hungry tummy.

Do get the kids involved too: if they help you chop vegetables, stir sauces, and weigh ingredients (all under supervision of course!), they'll be more excited about the food they are eating, and it will help them learn about ingredients and simple cooking techniques. They can also take pride in the homemade sticky gingerbread in their lunchbox, and the chocolate monkey milkshake they offer when their friends come round after school.

Every meal is covered—breakfast and brunch, lunchboxes, teatime, and dinner, with desserts, drinks, and snacks along the way—so you'll never be lost for dinnertime ideas again. And all the recipes are designed to make life easy and please both little ones and adults, so grab a plate and tuck in!

breakfast & brunch

banana, pecan, & granola yogurt pot

1³/₄ cups plain yogurt
3 ripe bananas, sliced
¹/₃ cup pecans
¹/₃ cup molasses sugar
³/₄ cup granola
1¹/₂ oz. semi-sweet chocolate, grated

makes 4 pots

This balanced breakfast will keep your children's appetites satiated until lunchtime.

Spoon some yogurt into 4 glasses. Top with the bananas, then add the pecans, molasses sugar, and granola. Spoon the remaining yogurt over the top, then sprinkle with the chocolate and serve.

frozen berry yogurt cup

1¹/₄ lbs. frozen mixed berries
¹/₂ cup cane sugar
2 cups natural Greek yogurt

makes 4 pots

During the winter months, summery berries will remind children of days spent playing in the garden. They're also a great source of vitamin C.

Put the frozen berries in a blender with the sugar and blitz into small pieces. Take 4 glasses and fill with alternating layers of yogurt and berries. Let sit for 5 minutes before serving.

muesli

¹/₄ cup sunflower seeds

¹/₄ cup pumpkin seeds

2 tablespoons flaxseed (optional)

¹/₃ cup slivered almonds

¹/₃ cup hazelnuts, chopped

3 cups old-fashioned rolled oats

¹/₄ cup wheat germ (optional)

¹/₄ cup dried apricots, chopped

¹/₄ cup dried banana

¹/₄ cup golden raisins

¹/₄ cup dried cherries or cranberries

To serve:

1 banana, sliced, or a small handful of
    fresh berries or seedless grapes

cold milk or plain yogurt

2 baking sheets

makes 2 lbs.

The nuts and seeds in this muesli are full of vitamins and minerals, the oats provide slow-releasing energy, and the fruit fiber. You couldn't give your kids a better start to the day.

Preheat the oven to 400°F.

Sprinkle all the seeds and nuts on one baking sheet and the oats on another. Cook in the preheated oven for 10–15 minutes or until lightly toasted then let cool.

Once cool, put the nuts, seeds, and oats in a large airtight container. Add the wheat germ (if using) and dried fruit, then close the lid securely and shake well. Store in a cool dry place.

To serve, spoon about 5 tablespoons muesli into a bowl, top with fresh fruit, and pour over some milk or add some plain yogurt.

VARIATION

To make granola, put all the ingredients listed above in a bowl and add 2 tablespoons maple syrup. Mix well. Transfer to a nonstick baking sheet and bake in a preheated oven at 325°F for about 40 minutes, stirring halfway through, until crisp and golden. Serve with cold milk or plain yogurt.

pink porridge

½ cup old-fashioned rolled oats

2 tablespoons wheat germ (optional)

2½ cups milk (see Cook's Tip)

½ cup raspberries or strawberries, hulled, plus extra for serving

1–2 teaspoon honey (optional)

serves 2–4

Oats are an excellent source of slow-releasing sugars, fiber, iron, zinc, and B vitamins. The fresh fruit adds a gloriously kid-friendly pink tinge!

Put the oats, wheat germ, if using, and milk in a large microwaveable bowl and cover with microwaveable plastic wrap. Pierce the plastic wrap and heat in a microwave on HIGH for 4–5 minutes. Stir and let stand for 2 minutes.

Transfer the porridge to a blender, add the fruit, and process until smooth. Add honey, if using, to taste. If necessary, return the porridge to the microwaveable bowl and reheat on HIGH for 1 minute.

To serve, spoon into individual bowls and top with a few whole strawberries or raspberries.

COOK'S TIP

Use whole milk for children under the age of 5, lowfat milk for children over 5.

VARIATION

Replace the raspberries or strawberries with 1 sliced banana and ½ teaspoon ground cinnamon.

scrambled eggs

6 eggs
4 tablespoons milk
2 tablespoons butter
sea salt and freshly ground
   black pepper
freshly chopped chives, to serve

serves 4

Make these scrambled eggs in the microwave or on the stovetop in a nonstick pan for a creamier, more comforting texture.

Whisk the eggs together with the milk and seasoning. Melt the butter in a medium nonstick pan, then add the egg mixture, stirring frequently until it reaches a creamy consistency. Serve with a sprinkling of chopped chives and hot buttered toast. For a real treat add a few slices of smoked salmon.

poached eggs

4 eggs

serves 2–4

Poached eggs are ready in just five minutes—perfect if you're having to fit dinner around a heavy timetable of extra-curricular activities.

Fill a large saucepan with boiling water. Crack the eggs into 4 cups, stir the water with a spoon and slip each egg into it. Bring to a gentle simmer, then cover with a lid, remove from the heat, and let stand: 5 minutes for soft poached eggs, and slightly longer if you prefer the yolk hard. Lift the eggs from the water with a slotted spoon and rest on paper towels to remove any excess water. Serve on toast, perhaps with a slice of ham underneath the egg.

scrambled eggs

eggs cocotte

2 oz. fresh spinach, chopped

4 eggs

4 tablespoons milk

³/₄ cup Parmesan cheese, grated

sea salt and freshly ground
    black pepper

4 ovenproof ramekins, buttered

makes 4

These iron- and calcium-packed baked eggs go down a treat at breakfast time or as a light meal.

Preheat the oven to 400°F. Divide the spinach between the prepared ramekins. Crack an egg on top, add a spoonful of milk to each, then season and top with the Parmesan. Place the ramekins on a baking sheet in the preheated oven and cook for 6 minutes.

omelet

6 eggs

6 tablespoons milk

3 tablespoons butter

sea salt and freshly ground
    black pepper

serves 3

Whether plain or filled with whatever you happen to have in the fridge, omelets are a great standby meal and a good, inexpensive way of ensuring that your kids have enough protein.

Whisk together the eggs, milk, and seasoning. Melt the butter in a large nonstick skillet, then pour in the egg mixture, using a fork to lift the set egg and let the liquid egg flow underneath. Cook until the top is just soft. Using a narrow spatula, fold over one-third of the omelet, then turn out and fold over again. Cut into portions and serve at the table.

whole-wheat banana & chocolate muffins

1²/₃ cups whole-wheat flour
2 teaspoons baking powder
¹/₂ cup cane sugar
¹/₂ cup chocolate chips
2 eggs, beaten
6 tablespoons vegetable oil
2 bananas
a 6-cup muffin pan, preferably nonstick

makes 6 muffins

The chocolate and banana in these muffins make the whole-wheat less noticeable. Children will gobble them up and get all the benefits of their high fiber, calcium, and potassium content.

Preheat the oven to 350°F.

Put the flour, baking powder, sugar, and chocolate chips in a bowl and mix well. Beat together the eggs and oil and pour into the bowl. Mash the bananas with the back of a fork, add to the bowl and mix together quickly: the mixture will be quite stiff. Take care not to overmix or the muffins will be heavy.

Spoon the mixture into the muffin pan and bake in the middle of the preheated oven for 40 minutes. Test for readiness by inserting a knife: the blade should come out clean. Eat warm or cold.

carrot & walnut muffins

9 tablespoons unsalted butter or
    polyunsaturated margarine
2½ cups all-purpose flour (or half
    and half all-purpose and
    whole-wheat flour)
1½ teaspoons apple pie spice
1 tablespoon baking powder
¾ cup light brown sugar
8 oz. carrots, peeled and grated
⅓ cup walnuts, chopped (optional)
2 extra-large eggs, lightly beaten
5–6 tablespoons lowfat milk
12 walnut halves, to decorate

Topping:
¼ cup lowfat cream cheese
2 tablespoons unsalted butter or
    polyunsaturated margarine
3 tablespoons confectioners' sugar
½ teaspoon pure vanilla extract
a 12-hole muffin pan, lined
    with paper cases

makes 12 muffins

These muffins are the perfect way to wrap up beta carotene-rich carrots and walnuts that are plentiful in omega-3 fatty acids in kid-friendly packages. Try not to overmix the muffin mixture as this can give the muffins a heavy texture.

Preheat the oven to 400°F.

Melt the butter in a small saucepan over gentle heat, then let cool slightly.

Meanwhile, sift the flour, apple pie spice, and baking powder into a large mixing bowl. Stir in the brown sugar, carrots, and chopped walnuts, if using.

Pour the butter into the flour mixture with the eggs and milk and mix gently with a wooden spoon until combined. Spoon the mixture into the paper cases, then bake in the preheated oven for 20 minutes until risen and golden. Transfer to a wire rack to cool.

To make the topping, beat together the cream cheese, butter, confectioners' sugar, and vanilla extract until smooth and creamy. Spread the cream cheese mixture on top of the muffins, then decorate each with a walnut half.

apple & oat muffins

3/4 cup whole-wheat flour

3/4 cup white self-rising flour

2 teaspoons baking powder

1 teaspoon apple pie spice

2 tablespoons wheat germ (optional)

1/4 cup light brown sugar

1/4 cup golden raisins

2 apples, about 8 oz., cored and
    finely chopped

2 tablespoons pecans, chopped

1/4 cup dates, chopped

1/2 cup sunflower oil

2 eggs, beaten

2 tablespoons plain yogurt

1 tablespoon sesame seeds

a 12-hole muffin pan, lined with
*   paper cases*

makes 12 muffins

These muffins are made with sunflower oil and yogurt, so they are moist without having the high saturated fat content of most commercially-prepared versions. Serve them warm on a cold morning or eat as a snack at any time of the day.

Preheat the oven to 400°F.

Sift the flours, baking powder, and apple pie spice into a bowl. Add any bran left in the sieve and the wheat germ, if using, and mix.

Add the sugar, raisins, apples, pecans, and dates and mix lightly with a wooden spoon. Make a well in the center, add the oil and eggs, and stir to mix. Add the yogurt and stir lightly, until just mixed (do not overmix or the muffins will be dry).

Spoon the mixture into the paper cases until three-quarters full. Sprinkle the sesame seeds over the top, then bake in the preheated oven for 15–18 minutes until firm to the touch. Remove from the oven and let cool slightly. Serve warm. The muffins can be wrapped and frozen for up to 1 month.

super-healthy blueberry mini-muffins

1⅓ cups whole-wheat flour

¾ cup white self-rising flour

½ teaspoon baking soda

2 teaspoons baking powder

½ teaspoon ground cinnamon

2 ripe bananas

2 eggs

⅔ cup brown sugar

6 cups polyunsaturated margarine

1 teaspoon pure vanilla extract

1 cup ripe blueberries

makes 20 mini-muffins

Your little ones will enjoy eating these for breakfast, as a snack, or for dessert with a spoonful of Greek yogurt or ice cream. They will also enjoy helping you make them as they really couldn't be simpler. They contain both bananas and antioxidant-packed blueberries. The quantities in this recipe are deliberately quite large as they freeze well.

Preheat the oven to 375°F. Sift together the flours, baking soda, baking powder, and cinnamon in a large bowl.

Peel the bananas and put them in a bowl. Mash them with a fork or purée them with a stick blender. Add the eggs, sugar, margarine, and vanilla extract and blend again. Pour into the flour mix, and mix until just combined.

Gently fold in the blueberries. Spoon into the mini-muffin cases and bake in the preheated oven for 25 minutes, or until risen and golden brown. Turn out onto a wire rack and leave to cool. Store in an airtight container for up to 3 days, or freeze.

blueberry pancakes

a little oil, for greasing

3/4 cup all-purpose flour

a big pinch of salt

1 tablespoon sugar

2 extra-large eggs, separated

2/3 cup milk

2 tablespoons unsalted butter, melted

6 oz. fresh or frozen blueberries

maple syrup, to serve

makes 12 pancakes

Not only are pancakes cheap and quick to make, they are universally loved by kids. Blueberries add a dose of healthy antioxidants to the batter.

Heat a nonstick heavy skillet over low heat.

Put the flour, salt, and sugar in a bowl and mix well with a wire whisk. Make a well in the center of the flour and pour in the egg yolks and milk. Using the whisk, mix together the milk and yolks, then stir in the flour gradually. The liquid will become quite thick, and you may need to whisk it more to get rid of the lumps.

Using an electric handheld whisk, whisk the egg whites until they are very stiff. Fold the whites into the other bowl. It is better to have small lumps of white than a completely smooth batter.

Turn up the heat under the skillet to medium/low. Add a large spoonful of batter to one side of the skillet—it will spread out to about 4 inches across. Drop about 6 blueberries into the center of the pancake. After about 1 minute, check to see if small bubbles are breaking on the surface of the pancake and it has begun to set. Flip it and cook the other side. Cook the pancake for another minute, then lift out of the skillet. Cook the rest of the batter the same way (try cooking 2 or 3 at once). Eat straight from the pan with any leftover blueberries and maple syrup.

buttermilk hotcakes
with bananas & maple syrup

2 cups all-purpose flour

1 teaspoon baking soda

2 teaspoons cream of tartar

1 tablespoon sugar

2 eggs

1 teaspoon sunflower oil

1¼ cups buttermilk

unsalted butter, for frying

slices of banana, to serve

a drizzle of maple syrup, to serve

makes 15–20 hotcakes

Kids will enjoy making these hotcakes as much as eating them, so get them involved. Don't be afraid to try out different toppings like strawberries and cream or blueberries mixed with Greek yogurt and a drizzle of honey.

Put the flour, baking soda, cream of tartar, and sugar in a bowl and make a well in the center. Add the eggs, oil, and half of the buttermilk to the well and gradually incorporate the flour with a whisk. Add the remaining buttermilk and whisk well to make a smooth batter.

Melt a little butter in a large, heavy skillet. Drop large spoonfuls of batter into the skillet from the tip of the spoon to form rounds, spacing well apart. Cook for 2–3 minutes until bubbles appear on the surface and burst, then turn them over and cook for a further 1–2 minutes until golden brown underneath. Put the hotcakes on a clean kitchen towel and fold it over to keep them warm while you cook the rest of the hotcakes.

Serve the hotcakes warm, topped with slices of banana and a generous drizzle of maple syrup.

cornish bread

1¼ cups milk

½ teaspoon saffron strands

4 cups unbleached white bread flour

1 teaspoon salt

2½ teaspoons rapid-rise active
dry yeast

1 stick plus 3 tablespoons unsalted
butter, diced, plus extra for greasing
the loaf pan

¼ cup firmly packed brown sugar

⅔ cup mixed dried fruit (sultanas,
raisins and currants)

a loaf pan (8½ x 4½ x 2½ inches),
greased with butter and gently
warmed

makes 1 medium loaf

By making your own bread, you can avoid feeding your children any of the preservatives found in commercially-prepared loaves.

Heat up the milk to hot but not boiling. Pour into a heatproof cup with the saffron, then cover and let infuse for 2 to 4 hours.

Put the flour, salt, and yeast in a bowl or the bowl of an electric mixer. Mix, then add the butter. Rub it between your fingertips until the mixture looks like bread crumbs. Mix in the sugar.

Gently warm the milk. Make a well in the center of the flour mixture, then pour in the milk. Mix until you have a heavy, sticky dough. Knead the dough on a lightly floured work surface for 5 minutes. Mix in the fruit then lift the dough into the warm loaf pan, pressing it down to squeeze out the air bubbles. Put the pan into a large plastic bag and gently inflate the bag to make a tent, so the plastic doesn't touch the dough. Tie the ends closed, then leave in a warm place until the dough has risen to the top of the pan—about 1 hour. Preheat the oven to 350°F.

Remove the loaf from the plastic and bake for about 1 hour until golden. Turn out onto a rack. If the underside sounds hollow, the loaf is cooked. If not, bake for another 5 minutes. Let cool before slicing. Eat within 4 days or freeze for up to 1 month.

soups & snacks

minestrone with pesto

1 cup canned white beans, drained
   and rinsed
1 tablespoon olive oil
1 red onion, chopped
2 garlic cloves, crushed
2 leeks, diced
2 carrots, diced
2 celery ribs, diced
6 cups chicken or vegetable stock
4 thick slices bacon, diced
1½ tablespoons tomato concentrate
1 bay leaf
a small bunch of fresh thyme
½ cup tiny pasta

Pesto:
½ cup pine nuts
a generous bunch of fresh basil
2½ oz. Parmesan cheese, grated
2 garlic cloves, crushed
6 tablespoons olive oil

serves 4

This hearty soup will warm up your children's stomachs after a wintry day spent playing with their friends outdoors.

Heat the oil in a saucepan, add the onion, garlic, leeks, carrots, celery, and diced bacon, and sauté for 10 minutes over medium heat without browning. Add the beans, stock, tomato concentrate, and herbs, bring to a boil, and simmer for 25 minutes.

Meanwhile, make the pesto. Put all the ingredients in a blender or food processor and whiz until smooth. Transfer to a jar, cover with olive oil, and store in the refrigerator until needed.

When the soup has finished its first simmering, add the pasta and simmer again for 8 minutes, stirring frequently. Season and serve with a spoonful of pesto and lots of crusty bread.

pumpkin soup

1 pie pumpkin, about 2 lbs.

1 tablespoon olive oil

1 potato, about 6 oz., diced

1 onion, chopped

1–2 garlic cloves, crushed

1 teaspoon ground cumin

4 cups organic vegetable or
    chicken broth

1 tablespoon freshly chopped
    sage leaves

²/₃ cup sour cream

To serve, your choice of:

freshly grated nutmeg

finely grated Gruyère or Cheddar
    cheese

roasted pumpkin seeds

croutons

serves 6

This is a really filling, warming soup. Pumpkin is also easy to digest, so it's ideal for kids who are recovering from short bouts of illness.

Cut the pumpkin into small wedges, then scoop out the seeds. Peel and discard the skin then cut the flesh into small pieces.

Heat the oil in a heavy-based saucepan, add the potato, onion, and garlic and cook gently, stirring occasionally, for 5–8 minutes until the vegetables are softened but not browned. Sprinkle in the cumin and cook for 1 minute more. Add the broth, pumpkin, and sage to the pan. Bring to a boil, reduce the heat, cover, and simmer gently for 20–25 minutes, until the pumpkin is soft.

Remove the pan from the heat and let cool slightly. Transfer the mixture to a blender or food processor and blend, in batches if necessary, to form a smooth purée.

Return the purée to the pan and heat gently. Stir in the sour cream, then ladle into warm bowls. Serve sprinkled with freshly grated nutmeg, cheese, roasted pumpkin seeds, or croutons.

creamy pea soup

3 tablespoons extra virgin olive oil,
    plus extra to serve
1 small onion, finely chopped
1 garlic clove, crushed
1 small potato (about 3 oz.),
    finely chopped
5 cups peas (fresh or frozen)
4 cups well-flavored vegetable or
    chicken broth
3 tablespoons heavy cream
sea salt and freshly ground
    black pepper

serves 4

This creamy, dreamy soup can be made with
frozen peas, so it's quick to prepare as well as
being packed with vitamins A, C, and B9.

Heat the olive oil in a large saucepan, then add the onion,
garlic, and potato. Cook over gentle heat for 8–10 minutes,
stirring regularly, until the onion is translucent and the potatoes
are starting to soften.

Pour in the peas and the stock. Let the soup simmer for about
20 minutes, until the potato is very soft.

Remove the saucepan from the heat and liquidize the soup with
a stick blender until it is smooth. If you don't have a stick blender
and are using a food processor or blender, let the soup cool
a little before you blend it.

Once the soup is smooth, stir in the cream and season to
taste with a little sea salt and some freshly ground black pepper.
Spoon into warmed soup bowls, garnish with a drizzle of extra
virgin olive oil, and serve with some good crusty bread.

alphabet soup

4 oz. smoked pancetta, cut into cubes

1 tablespoon olive oil

½ onion, chopped

1 large potato, cubed and rinsed

1 carrot, chopped

2 celery ribs, sliced

2 small zucchini, chopped

3 tomatoes, seeded and chopped

1 quart chicken broth

3–4 cups alfabetto or other small
    soup pasta

½ small round cabbage, sliced

1 cup green beans, cut into 1-inch
    lengths

1 cup peas, fresh or frozen

1 cup canned beans, such as
    cannellini, rinsed and drained

salt and freshly ground black pepper

To serve:

2 tablespoons freshly chopped parsley

crusty Italian bread

freshly grated Cheddar cheese

serves 4

This soup is a children's favorite and a sneaky way of getting them to eat their greens. The addition of legumes makes for a filling dish.

Put the pancetta in a large saucepan, heat gently, and sauté until the fat runs. Add the olive oil, heat briefly, then add the onion and cook gently until softened but not browned.

Add the potato, carrot, celery, zucchini, tomatoes, and salt and pepper. Add the stock and the pasta and heat until simmering. Cook over low heat for about 15 minutes. Add the cabbage and beans, bring to a boil, and cook for 5 minutes, then add the peas and canned beans and cook for another 2–3 minutes until all the vegetables are tender. Add salt and pepper to taste, sprinkle with parsley, then serve with bread and cheese (shown here melted on top of the bread).

COOK'S TIP

If your children refuse to eat any soups with "bits" in, cook the pasta and soup separately. Blend the soup element to a purée, then serve in bowls with a big spoonful of the pasta alphabets on top for them to stir in themselves.

sweet & spicy soup

1 onion, finely chopped

2 potatoes, cubed and rinsed

2 oz. dried apricots, chopped

1/2 cup split red lentils

1 lemon

3 cups vegetable stock

1/4 teaspoon ground cumin

salt and freshly ground black pepper

1 teaspoon extra virgin olive oil or a
    small piece of unsalted butter,
    to finish

serves 4–6

This family favorite makes a good meal on a cold day. It is full of wonderful flavors—savory, sweet, spicy, and aromatic.

Put the onion, potatoes, apricots, and lentils in a large, heavy saucepan. Juice one half of the lemon and add to the pan. Pour in the stock, then add the cumin, salt, and pepper. Mix well.

Put the pan over medium heat and bring to a boil. Stir, then cover the pan, turn down the heat, and simmer for 30 minutes. Stir the pan every 10 minutes to stop the lentils sticking.

Remove the saucepan from the heat and liquidize the soup with a stick blender until it is smooth. If you don't have a stick blender and are using a food processor or blender, let the soup cool a little before you blend it.

Pour the soup back into the pan. Taste and add more lemon juice, salt, pepper, or cumin as needed. Gently reheat the soup—be careful, because it can splutter as it comes to a boil. Turn off the heat and stir in the oil or butter and serve. Leftover soup will keep in the refrigerator for up to 4 days.

whole-wheat breadsticks with avocado & tomato dip

1½ cups whole-wheat flour

½ cup plus 1 tablespoon white
   bread flour

½ sachet (2 teaspoons) fast action
   dried yeast

2 teaspoons light brown sugar

1 tablespoon extra virgin olive oil

⅔ cup warm water

Avocado & tomato dip:

1 small ripe avocado

1 small garlic clove (optional)

1 tablespoon plain yogurt or
   cream cheese

1 very ripe tomato, diced

2 large baking sheets, lightly greased

makes 10–12, depending on size

Small children often need snacks to keep them going. These breadsticks contain energy-yielding carbohydrates, making them ideal.

Sift the flours in a large mixing bowl (adding the bran left in the strainer) and stir in the yeast and sugar. Make a well in the center and pour in the olive oil then gradually add the warm water, mixing the flour into the liquid. Mix to form a smooth dough.

Turn out the dough on a lightly floured surface and knead until it feels firm and elastic. Shape into 10–12 balls. Roll into sticks about 3 inches x ½ inch. Arrange on baking sheets spaced well apart. Cover with lightly oiled plastic wrap and leave in a warm place for at least 1 hour, or until doubled in size.

Preheat the oven to 450°F.

Dust the breadsticks with a little white flour and bake in the preheated oven for 12–15 minutes, or until golden brown. Remove from the oven and let cool on a wire rack.

To make the avocado and tomato dip, blend all of the ingredients in a food processor until smooth, then eat immediately with the warm breadsticks. The breadsticks will keep in an airtight container for up to 3 days.

cheese straws

5 tablespoons whole-wheat flour

5 tablespoons all-purpose flour

½ cup Parmesan cheese, finely grated

¾ cup mild Cheddar cheese,
    finely grated

a pinch of cayenne pepper

6½ tablespoons unsalted butter,
    cubed

1 egg yolk

1 large baking sheet, lightly greased and
    covered with baking parchment

makes about 20 straws

These cheese straws are rich in calcium, which helps keep bones strong. They are easy to make so get the children involved.

Preheat the oven to 400°F.

Combine the flours, Parmesan, Cheddar, and cayenne pepper in a large mixing bowl and rub in the butter until the mixture resembles fine bread crumbs. Add the egg yolk and mix until the dough comes together.

Roll out the dough on a lightly floured surface until you have a square about ¼ inch thick. Cut into long strips or straws and place on the baking sheet, leaving a small space between each straw. Bake in the preheated oven for 8–12 minutes, until golden.

Remove from the oven and transfer to a wire rack to cool. Store in an airtight container for 3–4 days. Serve with tomato salsa.

VARIATION

Add a heaping teaspoon dried mixed herbs to the flour.

puff pinwheels

4 strips of bacon

1 tablespoon olive oil

2 scallions, finely chopped

13 oz. ready-rolled puff pastry dough, thawed if frozen

2–3 tablespoons red pesto

1 cup Cheddar cheese, grated

makes 20 pinwheels

Liven up your child's lunchbox with these puff pastry pinwheels instead of a sandwich. Children seem to really like pesto, but if you don't have any in your pantry, you can try them without.

Preheat the oven to 375°F.

Cut the bacon into small pieces. Heat the oil in a skillet and fry the bacon for 5–10 minutes, until cooked. Add the scallions and cook gently until they are soft. Let cool slightly.

Unroll the pastry sheet, spread with the red pesto and scatter over the bacon and scallions. Top with the grated Cheddar. Carefully roll the pastry, starting with a long side so that you end up with a long, thin sausage shape.

Cut the sausage shape into 20 circles and put onto a baking sheet. Bake in the preheated oven for 10–12 minutes until risen and golden. Remove from the oven and let cool on a wire rack.

sausage & red pepper rolls

all-purpose flour, for dusting

13 oz. ready-rolled puff pastry dough, thawed if frozen

1 tablespoon olive oil

1 onion, finely chopped

1 red bell pepper, seeded and finely chopped

1 apple, cored and finely chopped

1 lb. good-quality pork sausage meat

1 handful fresh parsley, chopped (optional)

freshly ground black pepper

1 egg, beaten

2 large baking sheets, greased

makes 18–20 rolls

Alternative filling:

1 lb. ground chicken,
  1 tablespoon honey and
  2 teaspoons whole-grain mustard

Sausage rolls are a children's party classic. The red pepper gives them a colorful twist also contains beta-carotene and vitamin C.

Preheat the oven to 400°F.

Unroll the dough on a dusted work surface until it is approximately 12 x 11 inches and then cut in half lengthwise.

Heat the oil in a skillet, add the onion and pepper, and sauté for 5 minutes or until soft. Add the chopped apple and cook for 1 minute. Let cool slightly.

Put the sausage meat into a bowl, add the onion mixture and parsley (if using), season with black pepper, and mix together.

Divide the sausage meat into two and shape each half into a long sausage shape. Place each sausage shape along the long edge of each piece of pastry. Brush the opposite edge of the pastry with beaten egg and roll up from the sausage meat edge. Seal the pastry edges and turn the rolls over so the seam is underneath.

Cut each roll into 1-inch lengths. Cut a small slit in the top of each roll, brush with beaten egg, and pop onto the baking sheets. Bake for 20–25 minutes. Remove from the oven, transfer to a wire rack, and let cool.

vegetable mini-frittatas

8 extra-large eggs

½ cup light cream

freshly ground black pepper

2 tablespoons olive oil

4 scallions, thinly sliced

3 zucchini, chopped into
   ½-inch pieces

1 red bell pepper, seeded and chopped
   into ½-inch pieces

1 cup loose-packed soft sun-dried
   tomatoes, chopped into ½-inch
   pieces

4 oz. Fontina cheese (or Gruyère
   or Swiss cheese), chopped into
   ½-inch pieces

a good pinch of dried oregano

*a 12-hole muffin pan, well greased
   or 12 flexible muffin molds*

makes 12 mini-frittatas

These funsize, eggy frittatas are colorful and quick to make. The vegetables can be substituted with what's in season.

Preheat the oven to 350°F.

Break the eggs into a bowl. Pour in the cream, add some black pepper, then gently beat the eggs and cream until combined.

Heat the olive oil in a medium skillet. Put the scallions, zucchini, bell pepper, and a good pinch of oregano into the skillet and stir well. Turn up the heat to medium and cook for 5 minutes, stirring regularly, until the vegetables are a light golden brown. Remove the pan from the heat and let cool for 5 minutes before stirring in the tomatoes and cheese.

Set the muffin pan on a baking sheet. Spoon the vegetable and cheese mixture into the holes, filling each one with an equal amount. Pour the egg mix over the vegetable mixture.

Put the frittatas in the preheated oven to bake for 25 minutes, until puffed, golden, and set. Let cool for 5 minutes then gently run a round-bladed knife around the inside of each muffin hole. Carefully lift out or tip out onto a serving platter. Serve warm or at room temperature.

cornbread muffins

1½ cups whole-wheat flour,
  preferably stone-ground
1 tablespoon baking powder
½ teaspoon sea salt
¾ cup cornmeal
1 teaspoon cumin seeds
½–1 fresh red chile, seeded and
  finely chopped
2 tablespoons freshly chopped
  cilantro
½ cup fresh or frozen corn kernels
1⅓ cups lowfat milk
1 egg, beaten
3 tablespoons safflower oil
freshly ground black pepper
a 12-hole non-stick muffin pan,
  lightly greased

makes 12 muffins

Cornbread is a 'quick' bread that is a favorite with both adults and kids. This flavored version is made as muffins to serve with a bowlful of soup or a slow-cooked casserole.

Preheat the oven to 375°F.

Sift the flour, baking powder, and salt into a mixing bowl, tipping in any bran left in the strainer. Add a grinding of black pepper, then stir in the cornmeal, cumin seeds, chile, cilantro, and sweetcorn kernels.

Mix the milk, egg, and safflower oil together, then pour onto the dry ingredients and stir together briefly until just mixed. Spoon into the prepared muffin pan, then bake in the preheated oven for 20 minutes until risen, firm, and lightly browned.

Remove the muffins from the pan and let cool slightly on a wire rack before serving.

lunchboxes

smoked mackerel pâté

smoked mackerel pâté

3 smoked mackerel fillets
4 heaping tablespoons plain yogurt
1 garlic clove, roughly chopped
1 tablespoon whole-grain mustard or
    1–2 tablespoons horseradish
    (optional)
freshly squeezed juice of 1 lemon
freshly ground black pepper
fingers of toast or vegetable sticks,
    to serve

makes 4 small tubs

Mackerel has the highest omega-3 content of all oily fish. This pâté makes a good accompaniment to vegetable sticks or use it as a sandwich filler.

Remove the skin from the mackerel fillets and flake the fish into a food processor (or into a bowl if using a stick blender). Add the yogurt, garlic, mustard, and lemon juice and purée until smooth. Season with a little freshly ground black pepper, if liked.

Put the pâté into small airtight tubs and store in the refrigerator, ready to serve. It will keep for 2–3 days.

hummus

15-oz. can chickpeas, rinsed and
    drained
2 tablespoons tahini (ground sesame
    seed paste)
2 tablespoons freshly squeezed
    lemon juice
2–3 tablespoons olive oil
1 garlic clove, crushed

serves 6–8

This tasty dip contains lots of calcium and protein from the chickpeas and tahini, as well as iron, fiber, and magnesium.

Put all the ingredients in a food processor and blend, using the pulse button, to form a smooth purée, about 1 minute. If the mixture is too stiff, add another tablespoon of oil and a little cooled boiled water. Serve with vegetable sticks or breadsticks for dipping. If not using immediately, cover with plastic wrap and store in the refrigerator for up to 3 days.

guacamole

2 ripe avocados, peeled, pitted, and
  roughly chopped
2 tablespoons freshly squeezed lemon
  or lime juice
2 ripe tomatoes
1 garlic clove, crushed
freshly ground black pepper

serves 4–6

Avocados have the highest protein content of
any fruit and are a good source of vitamin C.

Put the avocados in a small bowl, add the lemon or lime juice,
and toss well. Cut the tomatoes into quarters and remove and
discard the seeds, if you like. Put the tomatoes, garlic, avocado
pieces, and black pepper, to taste, in a food processor. Blend for
1–2 minutes until smooth. Transfer to a small serving bowl and
serve with vegetable sticks and breadsticks for dipping.

If not using immediately, cover the bowl with plastic wrap and
store in the refrigerator for up to 24 hours.

roasted root dippers

1 sweet potato
1 parsnip
1 carrot
1 potato
2 tablespoons olive oil
a selection of dips, to serve

serves 4–6

This is another great way to encourage your
children to eat more vegetables.

Preheat the oven to 375°F.

Peel the vegetables and cut them into thick, chunky chips.
Put them in a roasting pan, pour over the oil, and toss well to
coat. Roast in the preheated oven for 40–50 minutes, stirring
occasionally, until tender. Serve with dips of your choice.

super-easy sandwiches

It's often tricky to come up with sandwich fillers that are both nutritious and liked by children. Here are a few suggestions. They all make 4.

4 sesame seed bagels, halved

2–3 tablespoons lowfat cream cheese

4 thin slices smoked salmon

2 inches cucumber, sliced

2 tablespoons coleslaw, optional

Smoked salmon bagels: Spread all the bagel halves with the cream cheese. Put a slice of smoked salmon and some cucumber slices on four of the bagel halves. Divide the coleslaw, if using, between them, then top with the bagel lids. Cut each bagel in half. Wrap in plastic wrap or foil and store in the refrigerator until ready to pack.

4 whole-wheat pita breads

4 tablespoons hummus

½ romaine lettuce, roughly shredded

3 inches cucumber, thinly sliced

3–4 tomatoes, thinly sliced

1 carrot, grated

2 tablespoons Cheddar cheese, grated

Carrot & hummus pitas: Warm the pita breads in a toaster or under a hot broiler for 1 minute. Let cool slightly, then split them. Put 1 tablespoon hummus in each one. Half fill with lettuce, then add some cucumber and tomato slices and grated carrot. Add some cheese, then wrap in plastic wrap or foil and store in the refrigerator until ready to pack.

1 large avocado, sliced

2 teaspoons fresh lemon juice

1 tomato, thinly sliced

4 whole-wheat rolls, halved

2–3 tablespoons lowfat cream cheese

1 Boston lettuce, rinsed

4 oz. thinly sliced roast chicken

Chicken & avocado rolls: Put the avocado slices and lemon juice in a small bowl and mash to a rough purée with a fork. Add the tomato and mix well. Spread each half of the rolls with a little cream cheese. Put a couple of lettuce leaves and 1–2 slices of chicken on top of 4 of the halves. Top with a spoonful of the avocado mixture and put the bread lid on top. Press lightly together, then wrap in plastic food wrap or foil and store in the refrigerator until ready to pack.

falafel in pita bread

2 tablespoons olive oil
1 small onion, chopped
1 garlic clove, crushed
2 x 15-oz. cans chickpeas,
    washed and drained
1 teaspoon ground cumin
1 teaspoon ground coriander
a handful of freshly chopped
    cilantro or mint
2 tablespoons mango chutney
freshly ground black pepper
flour, lightly seasoned
lettuce, shredded (optional)
1 tomato, sliced (optional)

makes 12 falafel

Falafel is best served in pita, it's easy to eat, and tastes great. This is a very quick and simple version of falafel, and is a good way to encourage your children to eat chickpeas.

Heat 1 tablespoon of the olive oil in a skillet, add the onion and garlic, and fry very gently until soft for approximately 5 minutes. Tip the onion and garlic into a bowl, add the chickpeas, cumin, and coriander, then roughly whiz together with a stick blender.

Add the cilantro and mango chutney, and season with freshly ground black pepper.

Mold the mixture into 12 balls and flatten into patty shapes. Dip them in the seasoned flour so they are lightly coated. Heat the remaining olive oil in the skillet and fry the falafels on medium heat for 3 minutes on each side until golden brown. Let cool, then put into pita breads with the lettuce, tomato, and extra mango chutney, if liked.

meaty sandwiches

Leftover roast meat is ideal for lunchboxes as a slice of meat is 1 portion of a child's daily protein requirement. Each of these makes 1 sandwich.

Roast beef with horseradish & cucumber: Spread a tiny amount of horseradish over your chosen bread and top with 2 pieces of roast beef and a few thin slices of cucumber.

Roast pork with applesauce: Most children love this combo. Split a roll, spread with applesauce, and fill with slices or pieces of pork. The applesauce adds a wonderful sweetness and helps to bind the pork together.

Roast pork with chutney: If your child likes chutney, mixing it with a cold meat is an easy sandwich filler. Spread some chutney onto your chosen bread and top with 2 slices of pork.

Lamb with mint jelly & baby spinach: Spread some mint jelly onto your chosen bread. Top with 2 slices of lamb and some baby spinach leaves—a great source of iron.

Bacon with watercress & grated carrot: Finely chop 2 broiled slices of bacon and put onto your chosen bread. Top with a handful of watercress and grated carrot.

Broiled bacon with lettuce & tomato: With this combination, it works best if all the ingredients are finely chopped and mixed together, especially for younger children. Put 2 broiled slices of bacon onto some bread. Top with tomato slices and shredded lettuce.

Bacon with egg & tomato: Mash 1 hard-cooked egg, spread onto 2 slices of bread, sprinkle over 2 finely chopped broiled slices of bacon and top with 1 ripe sliced tomato.

sausage & chutney sandwich

1 good-quality sausage
chutney and bread of your choice

makes 1 sandwich

Leftover sausages make a substantial sandwich filler that's ready in minutes.

Thinly slice a cooked cold sausage. Spread some chutney onto your chosen bread and top with the sausage. If your child fancies something more exciting, try the sesame sausages below.

sesame sausages

12 good-quality chipolatas
2 tablespoons honey
2 tablespoons sesame seeds
a heavy-based roasting dish

makes 24 sausages

This is a quick recipe idea for sausages—great for lunchboxes, but also a big hit at children's parties. You'll find that adults love these just as much as children do.

Preheat the oven to 400°F. Twist the sausages in the middle and then cut in half. Scatter the sausages over the heavy-based roasting dish and cook in the preheated oven for 15–20 minutes, turning once. Drain off any fat. Add the honey and cook for another 15 minutes, turning a couple of times until the sausages are sticky and golden all over.

Sprinkle the sesame seeds over the sausages and cook for a further 5 minutes.

chorizo & cheese muffins

4 cups all-purpose flour

2 teaspoons baking powder

a pinch of salt

freshly ground black pepper

8 oz. Emmental, Gruyère, or
   Appenzeller cheese, cubed

4 oz. thickly sliced chorizo sausage
   (replace with ham or corn
   kernels if you prefer)

2 extra-large eggs

7 tablespoons unsalted butter, melted

1½ cups whole milk

*a 12-hole muffin pan, lined with paper
   muffin cases*

makes 12 muffins

These savory muffins filled with molten cheese and spicy Spanish sausage make a welcome change to the usual lunchbox sandwich.

Preheat the oven to 400°F.

Set a large strainer over a mixing bowl. Tip the flour into the sieve, then add the baking powder, salt, and a few grinds of pepper, and sift these ingredients into the bowl.

Add the cheese to the bowl. Using kitchen scissors, cut up the chorizo into pieces about the same size as the cheese. Add to the bowl and mix well. Make a well in the center of the mixture.

Beat the eggs with a fork until just broken up. Pour into the well in the mixture along with the melted butter and milk. Mix all the ingredients together with a wooden spoon to make a rough-looking mixture. Spoon equal amounts of the mixture into the prepared paper cases.

Bake the muffins in the preheated oven for 30 minutes, until golden brown. Remove the pan from the oven, let cool for a couple of minutes then transfer the muffins to a wire rack and let cool completely. Eat warm or at room temperature the same or the next day and store in an airtight container.

leek frittata

3 leeks, cut lengthwise then
   finely sliced
3½ oz pancetta, cut into matchsticks
2 tablespoons olive oil
8 extra-large eggs
a few fresh chives, snipped
sea salt and freshly ground
   black pepper
a crisp, green salad, to serve
*a round ovenproof dish with a diameter
   of about 9 inches*

makes 6–8 slices

Frittatas are similar to omelets and are eaten all over Italy. You can substitute the leeks for other seasonal vegetables such as zucchini, tomatoes, or fava beans and add some grated cheese.

Preheat the oven to 400°F.

Scatter the leeks over the base of the ovenproof dish along with the pancetta then drizzle with the olive oil.

Roast in the preheated oven for about 15 minutes, until the pancetta is cooked and the leeks are softened.

In the meantime, beat the eggs in a bowl until very smooth. Season with salt and black pepper.

Remove the dish from the oven and carefully pour in the eggs. Scatter over the chives. Bake for another 20 minutes, until the eggs are set.

Serve the frittata hot or cold with a crisp, green salad.

spinach & onion tortilla

5 eggs, beaten

sea salt and freshly ground
   black pepper

2 tablespoons olive oil

1 large Spanish onion, halved and
   thinly sliced

6 oz. (about 3 cups) fresh spinach
   leaves, washed and chopped

1/3–1/2 cup grated Cheddar cheese

makes 6–8 slices

Leafy green vegetables like spinach contain omega-3, an important fatty acid known to help concentration. Spinach is also a good source of potassium, calcium, and iron. Chop it up and add to omelets, pasta sauces, or fish pies—an excellent way of getting your child to eat greens.

Preheat the broiler to high.

Break the eggs into a bowl, season, and beat briefly with a fork.

Heat the oil in a large skillet with a heatproof handle and fry the onion until soft and pale golden. Add the spinach and sauté for a couple of minutes to wilt the leaves.

Pour the egg mixture into the skillet, turn the heat down to its lowest setting, and cook the tortilla, uncovered, for approximately 8 minutes, until there is only a little runny egg left on the top.

Sprinkle the grated cheese over the top and brown the tortilla under the preheated broiler for 1–2 minutes, until the top is golden and bubbling.

Use a palette knife to slide the tortilla out onto a plate. Cut into wedges. Let cool and store in the fridge, ready to serve.

chorizo & bean triangles

1¼ cups white beans, cooked
and drained

5 oz. chorizo, chopped

2 oz. Manchego or other hard
cheese, grated

1 tablespoon flour

1 lb. ready-rolled frozen puff pastry
dough, thawed

1 egg, beaten

sea salt and freshly ground
black pepper

makes 4 triangles

The chorizo sausage adds a lovely spicy zing to these triangles. This recipe is easy to follow so get the kids stuck in too.

Preheat the oven to 350°F, then lightly oil a baking sheet.

Put the white beans in a bowl, add the chorizo, cheese, and flour, season, and mix well. Pour in ¼ cup water and stir again.

Use the flour to lightly dust a work surface and unroll the pastry dough onto it. Cut the dough into 4 equal squares and spoon the chorizo mixture into the middle of each one. Brush the edges with beaten egg, then fold two opposite corners together to make a triangular shape. Press all round the edges to seal.

Place the triangles on a baking sheet and brush the tops with beaten egg. Make a small slash in the top of each triangle, then bake in the middle of the preheated oven for 40 minutes. They can be eaten hot or cold.

chicken & bell pepper stew

2 tablespoons olive oil

8 boneless chicken thighs

2 onions, finely chopped

1 garlic clove, crushed

2 red bell peppers, seeded and cut
    into bite-size pieces

1½ cups chicken or vegetable broth

1¼ cups canned cannellini beans,
    drained and rinsed

freshly ground black pepper

a pinch of light brown sugar
    (optional)

a heavy ovenproof pan

serves 4

You can make this recipe for an evening meal and then keep enough for the children's packed lunch the next day.

Preheat the oven to 350°F.

Heat half the oil in a heavy ovenproof pan, fry the chicken thighs until lightly browned all over, and transfer to a plate. Add the remaining oil to the casserole dish, then add the onions, garlic, and red bell pepper and fry gently for 10–15 minutes until very soft, but not brown. Add the broth to the mixture in the casserole dish and cook in the oven for 1 hour.

Spoon half of the sauce from the casserole dish into a bowl and whiz with a stick blender until smooth. Put back into the pan. Add the cannellini beans and chicken to the pan and cook for another 15 minutes until the chicken is cooked through. Cut the chicken into bite-size pieces.

Season with black pepper and a pinch of soft brown sugar, if you think it is needed. Serve for dinner and set some aside to cool for your child's lunch the next day. Wait until it has fully cooled, put in an airtight container, and store in the refrigerator.

tuna pasta salad

½ cup small pasta shapes

2 tablespoons pitted black or
   green olives or 2 tablespoons
   cooked corn kernels

2 inches cucumber, chopped

5 cherry tomatoes, halved

6 oz. canned tuna

a few fresh chives, snipped

Olive oil dressing:

2 tablespoons olive oil

1 tablespoon freshly squeezed
   lemon juice

½ teaspoon Dijon or mild mustard

a pinch of salt

a pinch of freshly ground black pepper

serves 2

"Bow-tie" (farfalle) pasta works best in this recipe and will entice the children. You could use cooked corn instead of olives if the children don't like strong flavors.

Fill a medium saucepan two-thirds full with cold water, then bring to a boil. Add the pasta, stir gently, then let boil until tender —about 8 minutes.

Strain the pasta, then rinse it under the cold tap, so it cools quickly and the starch is rinsed off. Drain thoroughly.

Put the olives, cucumber, tomatoes, chives, and tuna in a bowl.

For the olive oil dressing, put all the ingredients in a screw-topped jar, and screw on the lid. Shake well, then open the jar and taste the dressing—it may need a little more salt or pepper.

Pour the dressing over the salad, then mix everything very gently with a metal spoon. Cover tightly and store in the refrigerator for up to 48 hours.

creamy potato salad

1 lb. new potatoes, cut in half
   (about 3–4 cups)
2 tablespoons mayonnaise
1 tablespoon plain yogurt
a small handful of fresh mint or
   parsley, chopped
1–2 scallions, finely chopped
2 handfuls of cubed cheese or
   chopped ham if preferred
freshly ground black pepper

serves 4

If you prefer, you can make this salad with white cannellini beans instead of potatoes for added vitamins and protein.

Bring a small pan of water to a boil, add the potatoes and boil for 10–12 minutes until just cooked. Drain.

Mix together the mayonnaise, yogurt, and herbs in a bowl. Season with a little black pepper. Add the potatoes, scallions, and cheese. Mix everything together, let cool, and store in the fridge until needed.

potato, pesto, & tuna salad

1 lb. new potatoes, cut in half
   (about 3–4 cups)
2 large handfuls of green beans
   (about 5–6 oz.)
2 tablespoons green pesto
1 tablespoon olive oil
1 cup canned tuna, drained
a handful of cherry tomatoes, halved

serves 4

Canned tuna contains omega-3 fatty acids—great for keeping children's concentration levels up.

Bring a small pan of water to a boil, add the potatoes, and boil for 10–12 minutes until just cooked. Trim the beans, cut in half, and add to the potatoes 2 minutes before the end of cooking time. Drain thoroughly.

Mix together the pesto and olive oil in a large bowl and add the potatoes, beans, tuna, and tomatoes. Mix everything together, let cool, and store in the fridge until needed.

potato, pesto, & tuna salad

oven-roasted vegetables with chickpeas & couscous

2 tablespoons olive oil

2 garlic cloves, chopped

1 teaspoon sweet paprika

2 red onions, cut into wedges

1 large red bell pepper, seeded and sliced

1 small butternut squash, unpeeled, cut into wedges

6½ oz. cherry or grape tomatoes

3 oz. green beans, trimmed

2 sprigs of fresh thyme

1¼ cups couscous

1 cup cooked chickpeas, drained

finely grated zest and juice of 1 unwaxed lemon

sea salt and freshly ground black pepper

a large roasting pan, lightly oiled

serves 4

Roasting the vegetables will give them a sweeter taste, making them more child-friendly and ensuring they get valuable vitamins in their diet.

Preheat the oven to 400°F.

Pour the olive oil into a large bowl and add the garlic and paprika. Season well and mix. Place the prepared vegetables in the bowl along with the tomatoes and green beans. Stir until they are well coated with the flavored oil.

Put the vegetables in the prepared roasting pan with the sprigs of thyme. Cook in the preheated oven for 20 minutes, tossing them regularly to ensure even roasting. Reduce the heat to 350°F and roast for a further 20 minutes.

Put the couscous in a large bowl and add 1¼ cups hot water, stir well, cover, and let stand for 5–10 minutes. Meanwhile, put the chickpeas in a saucepan of boiling water and allow them to boil for 2 minutes. Drain and add the chickpeas to the couscous, mixing well to fluff up the grains. Add the roasted vegetables.

Put 4 tablespoons hot water into the roasting pan and mix well to combine with the vegetable juices. Spoon over the vegetables and couscous. Add the lemon zest and juice, mix, then serve.

coleslaw

1 small head or ½ large white
    or green cabbage
2 carrots, peeled and grated
1 red bell pepper, seeded and
    thinly sliced
a large handful of raisins
a large handful of peanuts (optional)
2 tablespoons mayonnaise or
    salad cream
1 tablespoon plain yogurt
1 tablespoon honey
freshly ground black pepper

serves 4

You may need to keep trying this recipe if your child turns his or her nose up the first time.

Cut the cabbage into quarters, cut out the core, and then thinly slice the cabbage and put it into a bowl. Add the carrots, bell pepper, raisins, and peanuts.

In a small bowl, mix together the mayonnaise, yogurt, and honey and season with a little black pepper. Add to the coleslaw and mix well. Store in the fridge, ready to serve.

NUTRITION TIP

If your child does not like eating cooked cabbage, making coleslaw is a good way of sneaking it into his or her diet.

lemon shortbread with berries

3/4 cup (1½ sticks) butter, softened

⅓ cup sugar, plus extra to dust

grated zest of 1 unwaxed lemon

1½ cups all-purpose flour

½ cup cornstarch

fresh seasonal fruit, to serve

an 8-inch square pan, greased and base lined

makes 10–12 fingers

A finger of homemade shortbread with some fresh berries is an ideal dessert for a summer lunchbox. If your children prefer orange, try adding the zest from one orange instead.

Preheat the oven to 375°F.

Beat the butter and sugar together until soft, pale, and fluffy.

Add the lemon zest, flour, and cornstarch and mix again until it comes together.

Cover the bowl and chill the mixture for 10 minutes, if you have the time. If not, you can cook it straightaway—it will not make a big difference either way.

Press the dough into the prepared pan and bake in the preheated oven for 15 minutes.

Remove from the oven and dust with sugar, if liked. Score the dough into about 12 fingers (score in half and then score each half into about 6 fingers) and let cool completely in the pan.

Once cool, cut into fingers and remove from the pan. Store in an airtight container.

date & seed bars

1 cup dried dates, chopped

1¼ cups old-fashioned porridge oats

3 tablespoons sunflower seeds
   (ground in a food processor)

1 cup whole-wheat flour

½ cup light brown sugar

1 teaspoon baking powder

⅓ cup hazelnuts, very finely chopped

8 tablespoons unsalted butter,
   softened

an 11 x 9-inch baking pan, greased

makes 10–12 bars

Children's tummies are small so it can be hard for them to get all the calories they need in just three main meals per day. These healthy bars will help boost their calorie intake without all the saturated fats, refined sugars, and additives often found in commercially-prepared alternatives.

Preheat the oven to 350°F.

Put the dates and ¾ cup water in a saucepan and bring to a boil. Reduce the heat and simmer gently for 20–25 minutes, or until the dates are tender and most of the liquid has been absorbed. Blend in a food processor until smooth. Set aside.

Put the oats, sunflower seeds, flour, sugar, baking powder, and hazelnuts in a bowl and mix well. Add the butter and mix in with your fingertips until well combined.

Put three-quarters of the mixture into the prepared baking pan and press down to make a smooth, even layer. Spread the date mixture evenly over the top. Sprinkle over the remaining oat mixture and press down lightly. Bake in the preheated oven for 20–25 minutes. Let cool in the pan, then cut into bars and serve. Store in an airtight container for 3–4 days.

cereal bars

⅓ cup plus 1½ tablespoons
    sunflower oil
2½ tablespoons light brown sugar
½ cup corn syrup
2½ cups rolled oats
¾ cup mixture of seeds (e.g.
    sunflower seeds, pumpkin seeds)
½ cup dried fruits (e.g. raisins, dried
    cranberries, or chopped apricots)
an 8-inch square pan, greased

makes 16 bars

These cereal bars contain far fewer additives and
sugar than store bought ones.

Preheat the oven to 350°F.

Put the oil, sugar, and syrup into a pan and heat very gently to
dissolve the sugar. Add the rest of the ingredients and mix well.
Tip into the pan and bake for 15–18 minutes until set and golden.

Let cool for 10 minutes, and then score into 16 bars. Let cool
completely in the pan, turn out, and cut along the marks into
16 bars. Store in an airtight container.

apricot slices

1⅓ cups dried apricots
approximately 6 tablespoons orange
    juice—you may need to add a little
    more during cooking
¾ cup sunflower oil
¼ cup honey
1¾ cups oats
1⅓ cups all-purpose flour (or a mixture
    of whole-wheat and white flour)
*an 8-inch square pan, greased and
    base lined*

makes 16 bars

Dried fruit is not only naturally sweet but a great
source of fiber to keep children healthy.

Preheat the oven to 350°F. Put the apricots and orange juice in a
saucepan. Simmer gently for about 15 minutes until the apricots
have absorbed the juice.

Gently heat the oil and honey in a pan until the honey dissolves.
Add the oats and flour and mix. Put half the mixture in the pan,
then cover with apricots and top off with the remaining oat mix.
Bake for 20–25 minutes until golden. Score into 16 slices while
still warm then cut once cool. Store in an airtight container.

hot dishes

pasta with ham & peas

10 oz. pasta, such as
    fusilli
1 tablespoon olive oil
1 shallot, diced
1 garlic clove, crushed
6½ oz. cooked ham, chopped
1 cup peas, fresh or frozen
    (no need to thaw)
6 tablespoons heavy cream
2 egg yolks
1 cup grated Parmesan cheese
sea salt and freshly ground
    black pepper

serves 4

This eye-catching dish is rich in flavor but low on ingredients. It's ready in just ten minutes. Get the children to join in with the cooking.

Bring a large pan of salted water to a boil, add the pasta, and cook according to the instructions on the packet until it is al dente. Drain and return it to the pan.

Meanwhile, heat the oil in a saucepan, add the shallot and garlic, and sauté over low heat until soft.

Put the ham, peas, and cream in another pan and heat to a gentle simmer. Remove from the heat and add the egg yolks, Parmesan, and seasoning. Mix well so that the egg does not scramble. Finally, add the garlic and shallot, toss through the pasta and serve.

zingy pasta

grated zest and freshly squeezed juice
   of 1 unwaxed lemon
1/4 cup light cream
1 tablespoon unsalted butter,
   at room temperature
1 cup watercress sprigs, rinsed
3 good pinches of salt
freshly ground black pepper
8 oz. thin pasta, such
   as spaghetti
1 cup grated Parmesan cheese, to
   serve

serves 4

A simple pasta dish that's ready in minutes, yet bursting with flavor. Serve on its own or with cooked chicken for extra protein.

Fill a large saucepan with water, add a pinch of salt, and set it over the heat to boil.

Combine the lemon zest and juice, cream, butter, watercress, and remaining salt in a bowl, then add some black pepper.

Once the water has reached a rolling boil, add the pasta and cook according to the instructions on the packet, until al dente. Drain and add to the bowl containing the zingy sauce. The heat of the pasta will warm the ingredients through and wilt the watercress.

Toss the pasta several times to coat it in the sauce. Eat immediately, sprinkled with Parmesan.

butterfly pasta with zucchini, raisins, & pine nuts

2 tablespoons golden raisins

3 zucchini, thinly sliced

2 garlic cloves, crushed

3 tablespoons olive oil

3 tablespoons pine nuts

grated zest of 1 unwaxed lemon

14 oz. farfalle pasta

1 cup grated Parmesan cheese,
   to serve (optional)

sea salt and freshly ground
   black pepper

serves 4

This is a family favorite. Children love the butterfly shapes but you can substitute them for any short pasta shape that you have to hand.

Put the golden raisins in a bowl and cover them with hot water. Leave for about 15 minutes, until they are nice and plump.

Heat the oil in a large saucepan and fry the zucchini over medium heat for 6–8 minutes, until they are golden. Add the pine nuts and cook for a further 2–3 minutes, until the pine nuts are golden. Add the garlic and cook for just 2 minutes; you don't want it to cook so much that it browns, as it will become bitter.

Drain the sultanas and stir them into the mixture together with the lemon zest. Season the mixture to taste with some sea salt and freshly ground black pepper.

In the meantime, cook the pasta according to the instructions on the packet, until it is al dente. Drain the pasta and toss with the zucchini mixture. Serve at once with Parmesan cheese scattered over it, if desired.

smoked trout & farfalle pasta

6½ oz. farfalle pasta

5 oz. naturally smoked trout fillet
   (or fresh salmon if unavailable),
   skinned

1¼ cups frozen peas

⅔ cup light cream

1¼ cups grated Gruyère cheese

a collapsible steamer

serves 2

This modern twist on traditional carbonara uses smoked trout, which contains healthy omega-3 fatty acids. The dish is ready in just 15 minutes—perfect for when the children are desperate for their dinner and you've had a busy day.

Cook the farfalle according to the instructions on the packet, until al dente. While the pasta is cooking, put a collapsible steamer on top of the pan and steam the trout for 8–10 minutes.

Remove the trout, flake it with a fork, and set aside. About 3 minutes before the pasta is done, add the peas to the pan containing the pasta water.

Meanwhile, put the cream and Gruyère in a saucepan and cook over low heat until the cheese has melted.

Drain the pasta and peas and toss with the trout and cheese sauce. Serve in warmed bowls.

niçoise pasta lunchbox

2 oz. whole-wheat pasta spirals
  or shells
4 oz. green beans, cut into thirds
1 egg
⅓ cup black olives
6½ oz. canned tuna steak in spring
  water, drained and flaked
1 cup cherry tomatoes, halved
2 small heads Bibb lettuce, leaves
  separated

Dressing:
1 tablespoon freshly squeezed
  lemon juice
1 tablespoon extra virgin olive oil
1 small garlic clove, crushed
2 heaping tablespoons freshly
  chopped basil
sea salt and freshly ground
  black pepper

serves 2

This lunchbox salad is bursting with color and virtuous ingredients. The whole-wheat pasta contains slow-releasing energy that will keep the children going until dinnertime.

Cook the pasta in a saucepan of lightly salted boiling water for about 12 minutes or until al dente. Add the green beans to the pan for the last 3 minutes of cooking time. Drain the pasta and beans, then refresh briefly with cold water.

Meanwhile, add the egg to a small saucepan of cold water. Bring to a boil, then simmer for 6 minutes. Drain and rinse under cold water until cool. Peel the egg and cut in half.

Whisk the dressing ingredients together with the seasoning in a mixing bowl. Mix in the pasta and beans, olives, flaked tuna, and cherry tomatoes. Divide the lettuce leaves between 2 bowls and top with the pasta and egg halves.

pancetta & chicken meatballs

1 lb. ground chicken

2 oz. thinly sliced pancetta,
    coarsely chopped

6 scallions, finely chopped

4 garlic cloves, finely chopped

2 red chiles, such as serrano,
    seeded and finely chopped

1/4 cup grated Parmesan cheese, plus
    extra to serve

1 tablespoon fresh thyme leaves

1 tablespoon olive oil

3/4 cup red wine

2 lbs. canned plum tomatoes

a pinch of sugar

10 oz. dried pasta, such as conchiglie,
    about 5 cups

sea salt and freshly ground
    black pepper

serves 4

This perennial children's favorite is made with chicken, pancetta, and herbs, making it lighter than the traditional all-meat version.

Put the ground chicken, pancetta, scallions, garlic, chiles, Parmesan, and thyme into a bowl. Add plenty of salt and pepper and mix well. Using your hands, shape into 24 small, firm balls.

Heat the oil in a large saucepan, add the meatballs and cook for about 5 minutes, turning them frequently until browned all over. Add the wine and simmer vigorously for 1–2 minutes.

Add the tomatoes, breaking them up with a wooden spoon. Stir in the sugar, then add salt and pepper to taste. Bring to a boil, then simmer very gently, uncovered, for 30 minutes until the sauce is rich and thick.

Meanwhile, bring a large saucepan of water to a boil. Add a good pinch of salt, then cook the pasta according to the timings on the packet, until al dente.

Drain the pasta and return it to the warm pan. Add the meatballs and sauce to the pasta, toss well to mix, then divide between 4 bowls. Serve topped with extra Parmesan.

parsley & pancetta cannelloni

2½ cups tomato purée

⅔ cup red wine

1 teaspoon brown sugar

1 garlic clove, crushed

1 bay leaf

1 tablespoon olive oil

12 dried cannelloni tubes

Parsley & pancetta filling:

2 tablespoons olive oil

1 onion, finely chopped

2 garlic cloves, finely chopped

4 oz. cubed pancetta

¼ cup freshly chopped
    flatleaf parsley

3 cups fresh white bread crumbs

⅔ cup heavy cream

grated zest and freshly squeezed
    juice of 1 unwaxed lemon

5 oz. mozzarella cheese,
    drained and cubed

sea salt and freshly ground
    black pepper

a baking dish, about 12 x 8 inches

serves 4

These cannelloni are bursting with a wonderful mixture of flavors. This dish reheats well so you can always make extra for the following day.

Preheat the oven to 375°F.

Put the passata, wine, sugar, garlic, bay leaf, and olive oil into a saucepan. Add salt and pepper to taste and bring to a boil. Cover with a lid and simmer for 15 minutes.

To make the filling, heat the oil in a saucepan, add the onion, garlic, and pancetta, and cook for 4–5 minutes until softened and golden. Add the parsley, bread crumbs, cream, lemon zest and juice, and salt and pepper to taste.

Spoon the filling into the cannelloni tubes and arrange the stuffed tubes in the baking dish. Pour the tomato sauce over the top and sprinkle with the mozzarella. Bake in the preheated oven for 40 minutes, or until the top is bubbling and golden and the pasta is cooked through.

pappardelle with breaded chicken & garlic butter

1 egg, beaten

3/4 cup fresh white bread crumbs

3 skinless chicken breasts

1/4 cup flour

3–4 tablespoons extra virgin olive oil

10 oz. pappardelle pasta

5 tablespoons butter

2 garlic cloves, crushed

a small handful of fresh flatleaf
   parsley, chopped

1 oz. Parmesan cheese shavings

sea salt and freshly ground
   black pepper

a large freezer bag

serves 4

Children will go mad for the winning pairing of breaded chicken and thick strands of ribbonlike pappardelle. Turkey or cod work just as well.

Put a large saucepan of salted water on to boil for the pasta. Prepare one bowl with the beaten egg and another with the bread crumbs. Put one chicken breast in the freezer bag and bash with a rolling pin until flattened out. Spoon some of the flour into the bag, season well and shake until the chicken is coated. Dip the chicken in the egg, then in the bread crumbs, and set aside. Repeat the entire process with the remaining chicken breasts.

Heat the oil in a large skillet over medium heat and add the chicken in a single layer. Cook for 2–3 minutes, then flip and cook the other side for the same amount of time, or until golden. When the salted water in the large pan is boiling, add the pasta and cook until al dente. Lift the chicken onto a cutting board. Add the butter to the skillet along with the garlic and parsley and cook over low heat until the garlic and butter are about to color. Season, cut the chicken into strips, and return to the skillet.

Drain the pappardelle (reserving a cup of the water), then put back in the pan along with the chicken and its juices. Stir well and add the reserved cup of water. Serve topped with Parmesan.

simple vegetable quiche

1 storebought whole-wheat pie crust

Filling:
3½ oz. broccoli, divided into
    small florets
1 tablespoon olive oil
1 onion, finely chopped
1 small red bell pepper, sliced into
    rings and seeded
1 carrot, grated
3 eggs
⅔ cup lowfat milk (use whole milk
    for children under 5)
¼ teaspoon freshly grated nutmeg
freshly ground black pepper

To serve (optional):
salad leaves
boiled new potatoes

serves 6–8

Kids love quiche and this meat-free version is
a great way of increasing your child's vegetable
intake. Almost any type of vegetable can be used,
so be creative. The eggs provide an excellent
source of protein, zinc, omega-3 fatty acids, and
vitamins A, D, E, and B12.

Preheat the oven to 400°F. Unwrap the pie crust and put it on
a baking sheet.

Steam the broccoli florets over a saucepan of gently simmering
water for 3 minutes. Plunge them into cold water and drain well.

Heat the oil in a nonstick skillet, add the onion, and fry gently for
5 minutes, stirring frequently. Transfer the onion to the pie crust,
spreading it evenly over the base. Arrange the broccoli, bell
pepper, and carrot on top of the onion. Put the eggs, milk, nutmeg,
and black pepper in a bowl and beat well. Pour the mixture over
the vegetables in the pie crust.

Bake in the preheated oven for 15 minutes. Reduce the oven
temperature to 350°F and continue to bake for about 20 minutes
until the filling is set. Serve with salad and boiled new potatoes,
if liked.

tomato, basil, & mozzarella pizza

Pizza dough:

3½ cups all-purpose flour

2 packages rapid-rise yeast

a pinch of salt

a pinch of sugar

1 cup warm water

2 tablespoons olive oil

Topping:

4 tablespoons olive oil

1 small onion, finely diced

2 garlic cloves, crushed

14-oz. can tomato purée

a pinch of dried oregano

8 oz. cherry tomatoes

2 mozzarella balls, sliced

a large bunch of fresh basil

sea salt and freshly ground
    black pepper

2 baking sheets or pizza stones

serves 2–4

Younger family members never seem to tire of pizza, so get them involved in the making as well as the eating.

Put the flour, yeast, salt, and sugar in a bowl, make a well in the center, then add the water and oil and gradually draw in the flour to make a smooth dough. Knead for 12 minutes on a lightly floured work surface. Return the dough to the bowl, drizzle with a little oil, then cover and leave in a warm place until doubled in size. This will take 1–2 hours, depending on the temperature.

To make the topping, heat half the oil in a medium saucepan, add the onion and garlic, and sauté over medium heat for 6 minutes. Add the purée, oregano, and the remaining oil, season, and bring to a simmer. Cook for 25 minutes, stirring frequently.

Preheat the oven to 375°F. Knock the air out of the dough and knead for 5 minutes. Cut in half, roll each piece into a ball, and let rest for 10 minutes. Lightly flour a work surface and flatten each piece of dough into a circle about 10 inches in diameter. Place each on a baking sheet and spread the tomato mixture on top, followed by the cherry tomatoes and mozzarella. Season and drizzle with a little extra olive oil. Put in the oven and bake for 12–15 minutes. Scatter with torn basil leaves, then serve.

charred vegetable pizza

1 zucchini, thickly sliced

1 small eggplant, cubed

4 plum tomatoes, halved

8 unpeeled garlic cloves

1 red onion, cut into wedges

a few sprigs of thyme

2 tablespoons olive oil

1 quantity Pizza Dough (see page 116)

6 oz. dolcelatte cheese, diced

sea salt and freshly ground
   black pepper

a handful of fresh basil leaves,
   to serve

2 baking sheets or pizza stones

serves 2–4

Children won't be able to resist this rainbow of vegetables, coupled with oozing cheese. You can always substitute the dolcelatte for mozzarella if your children don't get on well with blue cheese.

Preheat the oven to 425°F.

Put the zucchini, eggplant, tomatoes, garlic, red onion, and thyme in a roasting pan. Add salt and pepper and drizzle with the oil. Cook for 30 minutes, stirring from time to time, until softened and a little charred.

Lower the oven temperature to 400°F. Knock the air out of the dough and knead for 5 minutes. Cut in half, roll each piece into a ball, and let rest for 10 minutes. Lightly flour a work surface and flatten each piece of dough into a circle about 12 inches in diameter. Spoon the vegetables over the top.

Put in the preheated oven and bake for 10–12 minutes. Remove from the oven and top with the dolcelatte. Return the pizza to the oven and cook for a further 5–10 minutes, until crisp and golden.

Sprinkle with the basil leaves, cut into wedges, and serve hot.

fiorentina pizza

3 cups young spinach leaves

1 tablespoon butter

2 garlic cloves, crushed

1 quantity Pizza Dough (see page 116)

1–2 tablespoons olive oil

1 cup tomato purée

6 oz. mozzarella cheese, drained
    and thinly sliced

4 small eggs

½ cup finely grated fontina or
    Gruyère cheese

sea salt and freshly ground
    black pepper

2 baking sheets or pizza stones

serves 4

Spinach and egg is a winning combination on a pizza—it's also a great way of making sure your children get some iron and protein in their diet.

Preheat the oven to 425°F.

Wash the spinach thoroughly and put into a large saucepan. Cover with a lid and cook for 2–3 minutes, until the spinach wilts. Drain well and, when the spinach is cool enough to handle, squeeze out any excess water with your hands. Melt the butter in a pan and cook the garlic for 1 minute. Add the drained spinach and cook for a further 3–4 minutes. Season.

Knock the air out of the dough and knead for 5 minutes. Cut in half, roll each piece into a ball, and let rest for 10 minutes. Lightly flour a work surface and flatten each piece of dough into a circle about 12 inches in diameter. Brush with a little oil and spoon over the purée. Put the spinach on the bases, leaving a space in the middle for the egg. Put the mozzarella on top of the spinach, drizzle with a little more oil, and season.

Put in the oven and bake for 10 minutes. Crack an egg into the middle of each pizza, top with the cheese, and bake for another 5–10 minutes, until the base is crisp and the eggs have just set. Serve immediately.

herby trout triangles

8 sheets phyllo pastry
a little extra virgin olive oil, to brush
4 skinless and boneless trout fillets
1 scallion, freshly chopped
1 teaspoon freshly chopped cilantro

To serve:
boiled new potatoes
sugar snap peas

makes 4 triangles

This dish is a great way of getting kids to eat oily fish. Besides, it's good from time to time to expand their horizons and offer them something a little different from what they usually eat. You can use salmon instead of trout if you like.

Preheat the oven to 375°F.

Brush two sheets of phyllo pastry on both sides with olive oil and place them carefully one on top of the other. Repeat with the remaining sheets.

Put a trout fillet on top of a pair of phyllo sheets, and sprinkle over a quarter of the scallions and cilantro. Roughly roll up the trout, then fold the phyllo pastry over the trout to make a triangular package. Put the triangle seam-side down on a baking sheet and bake for 20–25 minutes until cooked through.

Remove the triangles from the oven and let cool slightly before serving with boiled new potatoes and sugar snap peas.

upside-down cheese
& tomato tart

½ slice of stale white bread

5 oz. Provolone cheese, thinly sliced

14 oz. cherry tomatoes

2 tablespoons olive oil, plus extra
   to grease

all-purpose flour, to sprinkle

10 oz. ready-made puff pastry dough

sea salt and freshly ground
   black pepper

a crisp, green salad, to serve

a 9-inch loose-bottomed tart pan

makes 4–6 slices

This attractive tart requires only a few ingredients and is ready to eat in just 30 minutes. The kids will find it fun to make too.

Preheat the oven to 400°F.

Lightly grease the base of the tart pan. Whiz the bread in a food processor until you get crumbs. Scatter over the the tart pan base. Arrange the cheese slices on top of the bread crumbs. Scatter with the cherry tomatoes then drizzle with the olive oil and season with salt and black pepper.

Roll out the pastry dough into a circle on a lightly floured work surface. Its diameter should be slightly larger than the tart pan. Lay the pastry over the tomatoes and tuck the edges into the pan.

Bake in the preheated oven for about 25 minutes, until the pastry is golden brown and risen.

Remove the tart from the oven and let cool for 5 minutes.

Place an upturned dinner plate (larger than the tart pan) over the pan. Carefully flip everything over so that the plate is on the bottom. Pull the pan away and the tart should slip out onto the plate. Serve sliced, with a crisp, green salad.

mini-meatballs & couscous with five-veg sauce

4 oz. lean ground beef

½ onion, finely chopped

1 oz. mushrooms, finely chopped

1 garlic clove, crushed

2 tablespoons fresh bread crumbs

1 teaspoon freshly chopped parsley

2 teaspoons vegetable oil

1 egg yolk, beaten

1 tablespoon extra virgin olive oil

2 cups couscous

3 cups hot chicken or vegetable broth

sea salt and black pepper

Five-veg sauce:

2 tablespoons extra virgin olive oil

1 small onion, peeled and chopped

1 garlic clove, crushed

2 carrots, chopped

1 small zucchini, chopped

2½ oz. mushrooms, sliced

14-oz. can chopped tomatoes

½ cup vegetable broth

1 teaspoon dried oregano

½ teaspoon brown sugar

serves 2–4

Not only is this ingenious little recipe quick and easy to make, it's packed with vegetables and children simply can't get enough of it.

Preheat the oven to 350°F.

Mix the beef, onion, mushrooms, garlic, bread crumbs, parsley, vegetable oil, egg yolk, and seasoning in a bowl. Shape into 12 mini-meatballs. Refrigerate while you make the sauce.

To make the five-veg sauce, heat the olive oil in a saucepan, add the onion and garlic, and sauté for about 3 minutes. Add the carrots, zucchini, and mushrooms and cook for about 15 minutes, or until softened.

Add the tomatoes, vegetable broth, oregano, and brown sugar, season to taste and simmer for 10 minutes. Purée with a stick blender, then leave over low heat to keep warm.

Put the couscous in a large bowl and pour in the hot broth. Cover and leave for 5 minutes. Fluff up the grains with a fork.

Lightly dust the mini-meatballs with flour. Heat the olive oil in a large, nonstick, heavy skillet and cook the mini-meatballs for 8–10 minutes, turning frequently, until cooked through. Serve with the couscous and sauce.

oven-fried chicken nuggets with potato wedges

2 cups fresh bread crumbs

1 teaspoon sweet paprika

¼ teaspoon dried mixed herbs
    or dried Italian herbs

a good pinch of salt

freshly ground black pepper

4 medium chicken breasts, skinless
    and boneless, sliced into strips

4 tablespoons unsalted butter, melted

a large nonstick baking sheet or roasting
    pan, lightly oiled

Potato wedges:

4 baking potatoes, scrubbed and each
    cut into 6 wedges

4 tablespoons olive oil

a nonstick roasting pan

serves 4

Make your very own healthier version of chicken nuggets. Serve with Thai sweet chilli dipping sauce or ketchup, if the children can't resist it.

Preheat the oven to 400°F.

Put the potato wedges in the roasting pan. Spoon over the oil and sprinkle with salt and pepper. Toss the wedges so that they are evenly coated in the oil. Put them skin-side down in the pan and bake in the preheated oven for about 1 hour, until brown.

Put the bread crumbs into a large, clean plastic bag. Add the paprika, dried herbs, salt, and pepper. Close the bag and shake well to mix. Dip each strip of chicken into the melted butter then put it into the plastic bag with the crumbs. When all the chicken strips are in the bag, close it tightly and shake it well so the chicken gets coated in the crumbs. Remove each chicken strip from the bag and put it on the prepared baking sheet, arranging the strips slightly apart and in one layer.

20 minutes before the potato wedges are ready, put the nuggets in the oven and bake for 15–20 minutes, until golden brown and crisp. Serve the chicken nuggets and potato wedges together.

nut burgers

8 oz. mixed unsalted nuts, such as
    cashews, walnuts, and peanuts

2 tablespoons olive oil

1 onion, very finely chopped

2 garlic cloves, crushed

3 oz. button mushrooms,
    finely chopped

1 small yellow bell pepper, seeded
    and finely chopped

1 cup fresh whole-wheat bread crumbs

1 carrot, grated

1 tablespoon freshly chopped parsley

2–3 fresh sage leaves, finely chopped

1 egg, beaten

whole-wheat flour, for coating

sea salt and black pepper

To serve:

4 whole-grain bread rolls

lettuce leaves

4 tomato slices

tomato ketchup

a baking sheet, lightly greased

serves 4–6

Nuts are a good source of fiber, essential fatty acids, and protein, making these burgers a healthier option for children than fast food fare.

Put the nuts in a food processor and blend until finely chopped.

Heat 1 tablespoon of the oil in a heavy-based saucepan, add the onion and garlic, and sauté gently, stirring occasionally, for 5 minutes or until soft and golden. Add the mushrooms and bell pepper and cook for 3 more minutes. Remove the pan from the heat and mix in all the remaining ingredients except the flour and the remaining oil.

Using your hands, bring the mixture together to form a large ball, adding a little water if the mixture is too dry. Shape the mixture into 4 burgers. Put the flour in a shallow dish and coat the burgers evenly with it. Transfer to a plate, lightly cover with plastic wrap, and chill for 30 minutes. Preheat the oven to 375°F.

Put the burgers on the prepared baking sheet and brush lightly with the remaining oil. Bake in the preheated oven for 20 minutes until golden and piping hot. To serve, put a burger in a whole-grain bread roll, top with crisp salad leaves, a slice of tomato, and a dollop of ketchup.

pan-fried mini beef patties with sautéed collard greens

2 tablespoons vegetable oil

1 small onion, diced

4 oz. lean ground beef

½ teaspoon dried thyme

6½ oz. potatoes, boiled for 12 minutes, then mashed together with 2 tablespoons unsalted butter

1 tablespoon freshly chopped parsley

1 tablespoon tomato ketchup

a dash of Worcestershire sauce

a little flour, to dust

a pat of unsalted butter

6 large collard green leaves, shredded

baked beans, to serve (optional)

sea salt and freshly ground black pepper

makes 12 mini beef patties

If your children like sausages and meatballs they'll love this. Get them involved in making this simple recipe too. The patties freeze well so make extra for busier days.

Heat 1 tablespoon of the vegetable oil in a saucepan and fry the onion for 3–4 minutes. Add the beef and fry for 3–4 minutes. Stir in the thyme and season. Cook for another minute.

Stir the mixture into the mashed potato with the parsley, tomato ketchup, and Worcestershire sauce. Let cool, then cover and refrigerate until cold.

Form the mixture into 12 mini beef patties, dust with flour, cover, and refrigerate for another hour.

Heat the remaining vegetable oil in a large skillet and sauté the patties for about 5 minutes, or until golden and cooked through.

Melt the butter in a large, heavy skillet, add the shredded collard greens and sauté for 4–5 minutes, stirring frequently.

Serve the patties and collard greens with baked beans on the side (if using).

lamb koftas with pita pockets

1¼ lbs. lean ground lamb

1 small red onion

2 teaspoons mild paprika

1½ teaspoons ground coriander

1½ teaspoons ground cumin

¼ teaspoon ground cinnamon

4 grinds of freshly ground
   black pepper

a good pinch of salt

a few sprigs of fresh flatleaf parsley or
   cilantro, snipped

Yogurt dip:

¾ cup plain yogurt

a good pinch of salt

freshly ground black pepper

a small bunch of chives, snipped

a few sprigs of fresh flatleaf parsley or
   cilantro, snipped

8 small pitas, to serve

16 wooden skewers

*a baking sheet or roasting pan, lined
   with foil and oiled*

makes 16 koftas

Children love eating with their hands and these tasty koftas are just the thing. In summer, pop them on the barbecue for an outdoor feast.

Preheat the oven to 425°F. Soak the skewers in a bowl of water to stop the wood from burning in the oven.

Meanwhile, make the kofta mix. Tip the ground lamb into a large mixing bowl. Grate the onion onto the lamb using the coarse side of a grater.

Put the spices, salt, and herbs in the bowl and mix. Divide the meat mixture into 16 even portions. Using your hands, mold each portion of meat around a skewer to make an egg or sausage shape about 4 inches in length and place on the prepared baking sheet. Cook the koftas in the preheated oven for 15 minutes, until well-browned.

While the meat is cooking, make the yogurt dip by mixing the yogurt with the salt and pepper. Mix the herbs into the yogurt then spoon the dip into a serving bowl.

When the koftas are ready, transfer the skewers to a plate and serve with the yogurt dip and warm pitas.

fish cakes

1 lb. white fish fillet, such as
    cod or haddock
1¼ cups milk
a handful of fresh flatleaf parsley
1 bay leaf
14 oz. potatoes, cut into large chunks,
    boiled for 12 minutes, then mashed
1 tablespoon finely grated unwaxed
    lemon zest
2 tablespoons freshly chopped herbs,
    such as dill, parsley, or cilantro
2–3 tablespoons whole-wheat flour
2–3 tablespoons sunflower oil
sea salt and freshly ground
    black pepper

Lemony green beans:
5 oz. green beans
1 tablespoon freshly squeezed
    lemon juice
1 tablespoon extra virgin olive oil

makes 8 small fish cakes

Even children who turn up their noses at fish will usually eat fish cakes. These are packed with quality fish and are completely additive-free.

Rinse the fish and put it in a skillet with the milk, parsley sprigs, and bay leaf. Bring to a boil, then cover and simmer for about 10 minutes until the fish is cooked and the flesh looks white. Remove the fish with a slotted spoon and transfer it to a large bowl. Let cool slightly then remove the skin and any bones and flake the flesh. Discard the cooking liquor.

Add the mashed potato, lemon zest, and chopped herbs to the fish. Season to taste with salt and pepper, then mix lightly. Using your hands, shape the mixture into 8 small fish cakes. Put the flour on a plate and coat the fish cakes in it. Transfer the fish cakes to a plate, cover lightly with plastic wrap, and chill in the refrigerator for at least 30 minutes.

To make the lemony green beans, lightly steam the beans for about 5 minutes. Drain, then put in a bowl, along with the lemon juice, olive oil, and a sprinkling of salt. Toss well and cover.

To cook the fish cakes, heat the oil in a skillet. Add the fish cakes and cook for 4–5 minutes on each side until crisp and golden brown. Serve immediately with the lemony green beans.

beef bourguignon

1 tablespoon extra virgin olive oil

1½ lbs. beef chuck or bottom round
   steak, cubed

2 onions, chopped

2 carrots, chopped

1 garlic clove, crushed

14-oz. can chopped tomatoes

1¼ cups vegetable stock

2 teaspoons freshly chopped herbs
   of your choice

1 tablespoon tomato paste

5 oz. button mushrooms

a pat of unsalted butter

6 large collard green leaves, shredded

sea salt and freshly ground
   black pepper

mashed potatoes, to serve

serves 4

The beef and collard greens make this an iron-packed dish. It may sound very sophisticated and grown up but children will love it too.

Preheat the oven to 375°F.

Heat the oil in a flameproof casserole dish. Add the beef cubes and cook until evenly browned. Remove from the dish and put to one side.

Add the onions, carrots, and garlic to the casserole and cook until softened. Return the beef to the casserole along with the tomatoes, stock, herbs, tomato paste, and some seasoning. Bring to a boil. Cover with a lid and cook in the preheated oven for 1½ hours.

Add the mushrooms and return to the oven, still covered, for a further 30 minutes.

Melt the butter in a large, nonstick skillet, add the shredded collard greens, and sauté for 4–5 minutes, stirring frequently.

Serve the beef bourguignon with the collard greens and mashed potatoes on the side.

goan shrimp curry

1 tablespoon ground coriander

½ tablespoon paprika

1 teaspoon ground cumin

½ teaspoon cayenne or hot chili
  powder

½ teaspoon ground turmeric

3 garlic cloves, crushed

2 teaspoons grated fresh ginger

8 oz. green beans, halved

1 tablespoon tamarind paste or
  freshly squeezed lemon juice

2 tablespoons coconut milk

14 oz. uncooked tiger shrimp,
  shelled and deveined

3½ oz. baby spinach, rinsed

sea salt and freshly ground
  black pepper

basmati rice or chapattis, to serve

serves 4

This quick curry will fill your kitchen with a
wonderful aroma as it cooks. If your children are
a little shy of spicy dishes, simply add less
cayenne or hot chili powder.

Mix the spices to a paste with a little water in a saucepan.
Stir in the garlic, ginger, and 1½ cups cold water, add seasoning,
and bring to a boil. Simmer for 10 minutes until the sauce has
reduced slightly and the raw flavor of the spices is released.

Meanwhile, cook the green beans in a separate saucepan of
lightly salted boiling water for about 5 minutes or until tender,
then drain and put to one side.

Stir the tamarind paste or lemon juice and coconut milk into the
spicy sauce base until smooth. Add the shrimp and cook for
about 2 minutes or until they turn pink and are cooked through.
Stir in the green beans and spinach and cook briefly until the
spinach has wilted. Ladle the curry into bowls and serve with
basmati rice or chapattis.

chili con carne

8 oz. ground beef

2 tablespoons extra virgin olive oil

1 onion, finely chopped

1 carrot, finely chopped

1 red bell pepper, seeded and
    finely chopped

1 garlic clove, crushed

1 tablespoon mixed dried herbs

14-oz. can chopped tomatoes

$^2/_3$ cup beef broth

sea salt and freshly ground
    black pepper

To serve:

white long-grain rice

nachos

guacamole

sour cream

serves 3–4

This dish is effective in boosting iron levels (the mineral most likely to be lacking in children and adults alike) as the vitamin C in the tomatoes increases the body's capacity to absorb iron from the ground beef.

Heat a heavy skillet and add half of the ground beef. Dry-fry over high heat to color the meat. Break up any lumps with the back of a fork. Repeat with the rest of the beef and drain off any fat.

Heat the olive oil in a separate saucepan and cook the onion, carrot, and red bell pepper until they start to soften.

Stir in the garlic and the herbs and cook for 2 minutes. Stir in the tomatoes and the broth and season well. Add the beef and simmer gently for 40–50 minutes until thick.

Serve with rice or nachos and a tablespoon each of guacamole and sour cream per person.

fish pie

1 lb. potatoes, cut into large chunks,
   boiled for 12 minutes then mashed
1 lb. cod or haddock fillet, rinsed
1³/₄ cups milk
1 bay leaf
8 oz. canned tuna in spring water,
   drained
2 hard-cooked eggs, roughly chopped
6 oz. baby spinach leaves, steamed
   and excess water squeezed out
1¹/₂ cups frozen peas, steamed
5 tablespoons sunflower oil
¹/₄ cup flour
1 large leek, thinly sliced
¹/₂ cup grated Cheddar cheese
sea salt and freshly ground
   black pepper
8 ramekins or 2 ovenproof dishes,
   2²/₃ cups each

makes 8 little pies

Protein, essential fatty acids, calcium, iron, fiber
—you name it, this fish pie has got it. Every bite
will help build fitter, stronger little bodies.

Preheat the oven to 375°F.

Put the cod, milk, and bay leaf in a skillet and bring to a boil.
Reduce the heat and simmer for 10 minutes. Remove from the
heat and strain off, reserving the cooking liquor. When the fish is
cool, remove the skin and any bones, then flake it. Add the tuna,
along with the chopped eggs, steamed spinach, and peas and
divide between the 8 ramekins.

Make the reserved cooking liquor up to 1²/₃ cups, if necessary,
with more milk or water. Heat ¹/₄ cup oil in a small pan and stir in
the flour. Cook over low heat, stirring continuously, for 2 minutes.
Take off the heat and stir in the reserved cooking liquor. Return
the pan to the heat and cook, stirring continuously, until the
sauce thickens. Season then add to the ramekins.

Heat the remaining oil in a skillet. Add the leek and cook for
5 minutes until softened. Divide the leeks between the ramekins,
then top with the mashed potatoes. Sprinkle with cheese. Bake in
the preheated oven for 20–25 minutes until golden brown and
bubbling. Serve immediately.

easy ratatouille & couscous

1 large green bell pepper, seeded
    and diced
14-oz. can chopped tomatoes
1 large zucchini, diced
1 eggplant, diced
1 onion, thinly sliced
1 carrot, diced
1 celery rib, diced
1 garlic clove, crushed
1 bay leaf
1 tablespoon finely chopped
    fresh basil
6–8 tablespoons freshly cooked
    couscous

serves 3–4

This ratatouille is packed with vegetables. It makes a versatile sauce and freezes well too— serve it with couscous or with pasta, potatoes, or rice. You can also try adding flaked canned tuna or fresh mackerel to it for extra goodness.

Put the bell pepper, tomatoes, zucchini, eggplant, onion, carrot, celery, garlic, and bay leaf in a large saucepan and bring to a boil. Skim off any sediment.

Cover and simmer for about 20 minutes, or until all the vegetables are tender and most of the liquid has evaporated. If there is too much liquid, remove the lid and boil briskly for a few minutes to burn some of it off.

Remove the bay leaf and stir in the basil. Let cool slightly, then serve with the couscous.

tarragon chicken casserole

4 skinless and boneless chicken
    thighs, about 11 oz., diced
2 large leeks, cut into chunks
2 garlic cloves, crushed
²/₃ cup chicken broth
grated zest and freshly squeezed
    juice of ½ unwaxed lemon
1 tablespoon freshly chopped
    tarragon, or 1 teaspoon dried
    tarragon
14-oz. can haricot beans, drained
    and rinsed
6½ oz. fine green beans
2 tablespoons sour cream
sea salt and freshly ground
    black pepper
a flameproof casserole

serves 4

As well as being extremely tasty, this casserole has all the fiber and lean protein needed to keep your children going. The garlic and leeks both contain potent antibacterial and antiviral properties too.

Season the chicken and dry-fry in a nonstick skillet for 3 minutes until browned. Transfer to the casserole. Add the leeks and garlic to the skillet with 2 tablespoons of the broth and cook for 2 minutes, then tip into the casserole.

Pour the remaining broth into the casserole and add the lemon zest and juice, tarragon, and haricot beans. Bring to a simmer, cover, and cook gently for 15 minutes.

Stir in the green beans, re-cover, and cook for a further 5 minutes until the beans are tender but still have some bite. Finally, spoon in the sour cream just before serving.

mozzarella-topped
herby vegetable loaf

8 oz. carrots, grated

1 red onion, finely chopped

2 garlic cloves, crushed

3 celery ribs, finely chopped

4 oz. mushrooms, sliced

1 small zucchini, sliced

1 tablespoon chopped parsley

2 tablespoons chopped cilantro

$^2/_3$ cup grated Cheddar cheese

2 eggs

1 cup whole-wheat flour

1$^1/_2$ cups mozzarella, grated

Sauce:

3 tablespoons extra virgin olive oil

$^1/_2$ onion, sliced

1 garlic clove, crushed

2 x 14-oz cans chopped tomatoes

1 teaspoon sugar

sea salt and freshly ground
    black pepper

*a 1-lb loaf pan, lined with parchment
    paper*

serves 3–4

Children can get involved in making this tasty, vegetarian loaf. It's packed with vegetables, ensuring a balanced meal.

Preheat the oven to 350°F.

Mix all the loaf ingredients except the mozzarella in a large bowl. Spoon into the prepared loaf pan and bake for 1 hour in the preheated oven.

Meanwhile, to make the sauce, heat the olive oil in a saucepan. Add the onion and garlic, cover with a lid, and cook over gentle heat until soft and pale golden. Add the canned tomatoes to the onion mixture. Stir in the sugar and season to taste. Cook, uncovered, for about 30 minutes, or until the tomato softens.

Remove the loaf from the oven and let stand for 5 minutes. Preheat the broiler to hot.

Tip the loaf out onto a plate and slice. Put the slices into a shallow, ovenproof dish. Pour over the tomato sauce and sprinkle with grated mozzarella. Broil for 4–5 minutes, or until the cheese is bubbling and golden. Serve immediately.

salmon skewers

1½ lbs. salmon fillet, cut into chunks

freshly squeezed juice of
   ½ small lemon

a small bunch of fresh chives, snipped

sea salt

1 lb. cherry tomatoes

3 tablespoons olive oil

lemon wedges, to serve

12 wooden skewers, about 12 inches long

a ridged stovetop grill pan

a pastry brush

makes about 12

These salmon skewers are especially tasty grilled on the barbecue, but you can cook them just as easily on a grill pan too. Salmon is a great source of healthy omega-3 fatty acids.

Soak the skewers in a dish of cold water for 30 minutes. This will stop them burning when you put them on the hot grill pan.

Combine the salmon, lemon juice, and chives in a large bowl and season with a little salt.

Push a chunk of salmon onto a skewer and then a tomato. Continue threading alternate pieces of salmon and tomato until you have just 2 inches clear at each end of the skewers.

Heat a ridged grill pan until quite hot. Brush the olive oil over the skewers with a pastry brush. Lay them on the hot grill pan and cook for about 5–6 minutes, until the salmon is cooked through and golden brown. Turn them over once halfway through cooking. You will need to cook them in batches.

Serve with lemon wedges.

desserts

berry berry peachy purée

berry berry peachy purée

½ cup frozen summer berries
1 ripe peach, pitted, peeled,
    and chopped
1 fresh mint leaf, chopped
1 tablespoon plain yogurt

serves 1

Berries are packed full of immune-boosting vitamin C and disease-fighting antioxidants. They taste delicious too, especially when mixed with some plain yogurt.

Put the summer berries, peach, and mint in a saucepan and simmer for about 5 minutes, or until the berries have thawed and collapsed a little. Let cool slightly, then press through a strainer into a bowl and stir in the yogurt.

little cherub's cherry semolina

6 sweet cherries, pitted
1 tablespoon unsweetened apple juice
1 ripe banana
1 tablespoon semolina

serves 1

This recipe combines delicious cherries and bananas with semolina to make it a little more substantial—perfect for breakfast or dessert.

Put the cherries and apple juice in a small saucepan and simmer for 2 minutes.

Peel and mash the banana, add it to the pan, and simmer for just under 1 minute.

Stir in the semolina and serve, or purée to the desired consistency using a stick blender.

fresh fruit jello

Orange jello:

1 packet orange jello

1 can oranges or fresh tangerines

Raspberry jello:

1 packet raspberry jello

1 can raspberries or fresh or frozen
    raspberries

Lemon jello:

1 packet lemon jello

1 can citrus fruits or fresh orange,
    peach, or apricots

Strawberry jello:

1 packet strawberry jello

fresh or frozen strawberries
    or raspberries

5–6 jello molds

serves 5–6

Jello is something all children enjoy, so why not put some in their lunchbox as a tangy treat? Add some seasonal fresh fruit or canned fruit to the pots before you pour over the jello. You can also make the jello with a mix of fruit juice and water.

If you're using canned fruit, melt the jello with the recommended amount of water. Then add the juice from the can of fruit and enough water to make it up to the right volume according to the packet instructions. If using fresh fruit, follow the packet instructions for the jello.

Mash half the canned or fresh fruit to a pulp and add to the jello mixture. Divide the remaining fruits between the jello molds. Pour the fruity jello mixture over the fruit in each mold and let set in the refrigerator overnight.

oatmeal pots with warm strawberry sauce

4 tablespoons fine or medium
    ground oats
3/4 cup whole milk
1/2 sweet apple, peeled and cored
4 tablespoons heavy cream
4 strawberries, hulled and sliced,
    to decorate

Strawberry sauce:
8 oz. strawberries
1 tablespoon freshly squeezed
    lemon juice
2 tablespoons sugar, or to taste

serves 2

This tasty dessert is full of berry goodness and will satisfy a sweet tooth without overloading your child with sugar. Adults will love them too.

Put the oats and milk in a small bowl and grate in the apple. Stir, cover, and refrigerate for about 8 hours.

To make the strawberry sauce, put the strawberries, $2/3$ cup water, the lemon juice, and enough sugar to taste in a heavy saucepan. Heat gently, stirring occasionally, until the sugar has dissolved. Bring to a boil, reduce the heat, and simmer for 5 minutes, or until the strawberries are really soft.

Purée the stewed strawberries in a blender, then strain to get a smooth sauce.

Divide the apple and oat mixture into 2 small bowls with a tablespoon of cream and pour over the warm strawberry sauce. Decorate with the sliced strawberries.

frozen fruit pops

2½ cups freshly squeezed fruit juice,
  such as orange, apple, or pineapple
  juice or 2 pints fresh ripe fruit, such
  as strawberries, raspberries, or a
  mixture of both
3–4 tablespoons superfine sugar
  (optional)
8 frozen treat molds

makes 8 pops

These juicy, tangy pops are a real summer treat for children and versatile too. They are full of the goodness of fresh fruit.

Set the freezer to rapid freeze. Rinse out the molds with cold water and put them in their rack.

If using fruit juice, carefully pour the juice into the molds, then push the handle tops into the lollies.

If using fresh ripe fruit, remove any stalks, rinse lightly, and cut any large fruit in half. Put the fruit in a saucepan, add sugar to taste, and ⅔ cup water. Cook over gentle heat for 5 minutes or until the fruit has collapsed. Let cool slightly, then transfer to a food processor or blender and process to form a purée. Sieve through a fine, nonmetallic strainer to remove the pips.

Make the purée up to 2⅓ cups with water or freshly squeezed orange juice. Pour it into the iced lolly molds, then push a handle top into each pop. Freeze for at least 4 hours until frozen. Use within 2–3 days.

ice cream sundaes

ice cream sundaes

2½ pints raspberries
4 scoops chocolate ice cream
10 oz. plain yogurt
1 pint strawberries, halved if large
8 scoops vanilla ice cream
2 oz. semisweet chocolate
    (at least 70 percent cocoa solids),
    roughly chopped or grated
4 tall sundae glasses

serves 4

No childhood would be complete without the experience of eating an ice cream sundae. These are packed full of fruit rich in vitamin C.

Put 1 tablespoon of raspberries in the bottom of each glass and top with 1 scoop of chocolate ice cream. Spoon over one-quarter of the yogurt in each glass, then top with one-quarter of the strawberries, reserving 4 of the strawberries to decorate.

Add 1 scoop of vanilla ice cream, then scatter over a little chopped chocolate. Add 1 more tablespoon of raspberries to each glass, then finish with 1 scoop of vanilla ice cream. Sprinkle with a little more chopped chocolate, top with a strawberry, and serve immediately.

sticky toffee & apricot sauce

1 cup dried apricots, roughly chopped
2 tablespoons light brown sugar
1 tablespoon butter

makes 1¼ cups

This wonderfully sticky sauce makes a fantastic accompaniment to ice cream.

Put the apricots, sugar, and ¾ cup water in a heavy-based saucepan. Bring to a boil, then cover and reduce the heat. Simmer for 12–15 minutes or until the apricots are really soft. Let cool slightly, then transfer to a blender and process to form a purée. Return the purée to the rinsed pan, add the butter, and heat gently until the butter has melted. Serve over ice cream.

lemon polenta cake

1½ sticks (12 tablespoons) butter, softened

¾ cup natural cane sugar

¾ cup polenta or cornmeal

½ teaspoon baking powder

1 cup ground almonds

grated zest and freshly squeezed juice of 1 unwaxed lemon

½ teaspoon pure vanilla extract

3 eggs

Syrup:

finely grated zest and freshly squeezed juice of 2 unwaxed lemons

¼ cup confectioners' sugar

a springform cake pan, 10 inches in diameter, lightly greased

serves 6–8

Children will love this sticky, syrupy cake. The polenta and ground almonds give it an irresistible texture. Serve it for dessert with heavy cream or for afternoon tea.

Preheat the oven to 350°F.

Beat together the butter and sugar until creamy. Add the polenta, baking powder, ground almonds, lemon zest and juice, vanilla extract, and eggs. Mix together until smooth. Spoon the mixture into the prepared pan and bake in the middle of the preheated oven for 30 minutes.

Meanwhile, make the syrup. Put the lemon zest and juice in a small saucepan with the confectioners' sugar and 2 tablespoons water. Bring to a boil and simmer for 2 minutes. When the cake is done, let cool slightly in the pan, then turn out and pierce all over with a fine skewer. Spoon the syrup over the cake, then leave for 20 minutes while it is absorbed. Serve with heavy cream.

freeform peach pie

Pastry dough:

1²/₃ cups all-purpose flour

a good pinch of salt

a good pinch of ground cinnamon

2 tablespoons sugar

10 tablespoons unsalted butter,
    straight from the fridge, diced

3 tablespoons cold water

Filling:

5 peaches, about 1¹/₂ lbs., pitted and
    cut into wedges

3 tablespoons superfine or granulated
    sugar, plus extra for sprinkling

a large baking sheet

serves 4–6

The appeal of this fruit tart is its rustic look.
Use slightly underripe peaches, pears, or apples,
depending on what the children prefer.

To make the pastry, briefly pulse the flour, salt, cinnamon,
and sugar in a food processor. Add the butter and pulse until
it resembles coarse crumbs. Pour in the water through the feed
tube and process until the dough comes together in a ball.

Gently knead the dough on a floured work surface for a few
seconds until smooth. Roll out the dough to a circle about 12
inches across on some parchment paper. Chill for 15 minutes.

Preheat the oven to 400°F. Sprinkle the sliced fruit with the
sugar and mix gently. Remove the dough from the fridge. Heap
the fruit into the center of the dough evenly. Leave a wide border
of dough, about 3 inches, without fruit. Gently fold the border
of dough over the fruit so the fruit in the center is uncovered,
leaving a gap of about 1 inch between the fruit and the fold, and
gently pinch the pleats of dough together every 3 inches. Try not
to press the dough down on the fruit.

Brush the pastry with cold water then sprinkle with sugar. Bake
for 40 minutes, until golden. Let the tart cool on its sheet for
10 minutes then slide off its paper lining. Serve while still warm.

summer fruit tart

2½ oz. semisweet chocolate,
    roughly chopped

Pastry dough:
12 tablespoons butter, softened
⅓ cup sugar
1 egg yolk
2 cups all-purpose flour, plus extra
    to sprinkle

Filling:
8 oz. mascarpone cheese
2 tablespoons sugar
2¼ lbs. mixed summer berries (such
    as strawberries, raspberries, and
    blueberries)
a 9-inch loose-bottomed tart pan
a pastry brush

serves 6

This tart is bursting with fruity goodness. The children will love the surprise layer of chocolate coating the pastry base.

To make the pastry, combine the butter and sugar in a bowl and beat until smooth. Add the egg yolk and beat again until well mixed. Stir in the flour and mix until you get a soft but not sticky dough. Divide the dough in two and freeze half for next time.

Roll out the dough on a lightly floured work surface until it is just a little bit bigger than the tart pan. Press the pastry gently into the corners of the tart pan and repair any holes with a little extra pastry. Trim the edges of the pastry case then pop it in the refrigerator for 30 minutes or so, to firm up.

Preheat the oven to 350°F. Take the tart out of the refrigerator and bake for 10–15 minutes until golden. Let cool.

Melt the chocolate in a heatproof bowl set over a saucepan of simmering water or in the microwave. Let cool slightly then brush the base of the pastry with the chocolate and let set.

To make the filling, put the mascarpone and sugar in a bowl and beat until smooth. Spoon it into the tart case, scatter the berries evenly over the mascarpone, and serve in slices.

seasonal fruit tray tart

1 lb. ready-rolled frozen puff pastry
  dough, thawed
2 lbs. seasonal fruit, such as apples,
  apricots, nectarines, peaches,
  or plums, cored or pitted,
  as necessary
1 egg, beaten
1/4 cup natural cane sugar
3 tablespoons butter
honey, for drizzling
confectioners' sugar, for dusting
a baking sheet, lightly greased

serves 6

A simple dessert that makes the most of any fruit in season. The children will enjoy getting involved with rolling out the pastry dough.

Preheat the oven to 350°F.

Unroll the pastry dough and place on the prepared baking sheet. Arrange the fruit on the dough in an even layer, leaving a 1 1/2-inch border around the edges. Brush the border with the egg and fold inwards all the way around. Sprinkle the fruit with the sugar and dot with the butter.

Bake in the preheated oven for 45 minutes, reducing the heat if the tart shows signs of burning. Drizzle with honey and dust with confectioners' sugar before serving.

baked lemon pudding

3 tablespoons unsalted butter

2½ cups granulated sugar

3 eggs, separated

3 tablespoons self-rising flour

1½ cups whole milk

¼ cup freshly squeezed lemon juice

1 tablespoon confectioners' sugar

a medium ovenproof baking dish

serves 6

This custardy lemon dessert will add a zing to the end of any dinner as well as filling the kitchen with lovely citrus aromas. It's cheap to make too.

Preheat the oven to 350°F.

Put the butter and granulated sugar in a food processor and process for about 10 seconds, until smooth. Add the egg yolks one at a time to the mixture and process for a few seconds after each addition.

Add the flour and process until smooth. With the motor running pour in the milk in a slow and steady stream, scraping down the bowl of the food processor with a spatula so all the mixture is incorporated and lump free. Transfer the mixture to a large bowl.

Using a handheld electric whisk, beat the egg whites until firm, then fold them into the batter in two batches using a large metal spoon. Quickly stir in the lemon juice. Spoon the mixture into the baking dish and bake in the preheated oven for 25–30 minutes, until golden on top.

Let the dessert rest for 10 minutes before dusting with confectioners' sugar to serve.

almond fruit crumble

20 oz. seasonal fruit such as apples,
  pears, plums, apricots, or rhubarb
¼ cup packed brown sugar
1 cup self-rising flour
1 teaspoon baking powder
1 stick (8 tablespoons) butter, diced
¼ cup natural cane sugar
⅓ cup ground almonds
⅓ cup old-fashioned rolled oats
a 1-quart ovenproof dish, buttered

serves 4

This timeless dessert is always a hit with children and adults alike. The crumble topping keeps well in the refrigerator so you can always double it up and put some aside for another serving.

Preheat the oven to 375°F.

Put the fruit in the prepared dish and add the brown sugar and 6 tablespoons water.

Put the flour, baking powder, and butter in a bowl and rub together with your fingertips until the mixture resembles bread crumbs. Stir in the sugar, almonds, and oats, then spoon evenly over the fruit. Bake in the preheated oven for 30 minutes. The crumble should be golden and the fruit bubbling up around the edges. Serve with cream or ice cream.

sweet polenta dessert

2½ cups whole milk

1¾ cups instant polenta

⅔ cup sugar, plus 2 tablespoons
  for the topping

⅓ cup mixed candied peel

⅔ cup candied orange peel

⅔ cup golden raisins

grated zest of 1 large unwaxed orange

3 tablespoons salted butter, plus
  2 tablespoons for the topping

2 eggs

sunflower oil, to grease

light cream, to serve

a baking sheet, lightly greased

a cookie cutter (optional)

a large ovenproof serving dish

serves 4

Children will enjoy this melt-in-the-mouth, comforting dessert. The addition of golden raisins and candied peel gives it a great texture.

Pour 2½ cups water and the milk into a large saucepan and bring to a boil over medium heat. Pour the polenta in a steady stream into the pan, stirring quickly with a whisk. Cook the polenta for the time recommended on the packet.

When the polenta is cooked, remove it from the heat. Stir in the sugar, peel, raisins, grated orange zest, and butter until everything is evenly mixed and the butter has melted.

Crack the eggs into a small bowl and beat them until smooth. Stir them into the polenta until everything is well mixed. Pour the mixture out onto the prepared baking sheet, then smooth it over with a palette knife. Let cool and set.

When you are ready to cook the polenta, preheat the oven to 400°F. Cut the polenta into circles using a cookie cutter or an upside-down glass and lay the circles in the serving dish. To make the topping, melt the remaining butter in a pan. Drizzle the butter and remaining sugar over the polenta circles. Transfer the dish to the preheated oven and bake for about 15–20 minutes, until golden. Serve with light cream.

brownies & ice cream

4 extra-large eggs

1½ cups sugar

1 teaspoon pure vanilla extract

1½ sticks unsalted butter, melted

¾ cup unsweetened cocoa powder

1¾ cups all-purpose flour

3½ oz. best-quality white chocolate, broken up into chunks

vanilla ice cream, to serve

a cake pan, 8 inches square

makes 16

Warm fudge sauce:

5 oz. bittersweet chocolate, roughly chopped

2 tablespoons unsalted butter

2 tablespoons corn syrup

½ cup whole milk or half-and-half

serves 6

A great mix-and-bake recipe with white chocolate lumps for those who don't or can't eat nuts. For a special birthday meal, serve the brownies warm with ice cream or the warm fudge sauce below.

Preheat the oven to 325°F.

Crack the eggs into a large mixing bowl. Tip the sugar into the bowl, then add the vanilla. Stir well with a wooden spoon for 1 minute until completely mixed.

Pour in the melted butter and stir for another minute.

Sift the cocoa and flour onto the egg mixture. Stir well for another minute. When there are no streaks of flour left, add the white chocolate chunks. Stir until just mixed, then spoon the mixture into the foil-lined pan.

Bake in the preheated oven for about 40 minutes. Insert a skewer halfway between the sides and the center—if it is clean, then the brownies are ready, if not, then cook for 5 minutes more. Leave to cool on a wire rack. When completely cold, remove the brownies from the pan then cut into 16 squares. Store in an airtight container and eat within 5 days or freeze for up to 1 month.

To make the warm fudge sauce, put the chocolate, butter, corn syrup, and milk in a small saucepan over very low heat. When the butter and chocolate start to melt, stir gently every minute or so to make a smooth sauce. Take off the heat and serve with the brownies. The sauce will keep for a few days in the refrigerator.

baked alaska

1 pint strawberry, raspberry, or
    vanilla ice cream
1 ready-made sponge base,
    8 inches in diameter
4 egg whites
1 cup plus 2 tablespoons
    superfine sugar
1½ cups or 5 oz. raspberries
confectioners' sugar, for sprinkling

makes 1 large cake

Children will love this kitsch dessert that is great fun to make and eat. Use a ready-made sponge for the base to speed up the process and top with your favorite ice cream.

Remove the ice cream from the freezer and leave until soft enough to spoon out. Put the sponge base onto a baking sheet, then spoon the ice cream on top to make an even layer. Put the whole thing back into the freezer and leave until very firm—at least 1 hour. It will keep for up to 3 days in the freezer.

When you are ready to finish the alaska, preheat the oven to 425°F.

Put the egg whites into a very clean mixing bowl. Using an electric mixer or hand whisk, whisk until the whites turn into a stiff white foam—lift out the whisk and there will be a little peak of white standing on the end. Quickly whisk the sugar into the egg whites to make a stiff and glossy meringue.

Remove the sponge and ice cream from the freezer. Top with the raspberries. Quickly cover the whole thing with the meringue, making sure there are no gaps. Sprinkle with sifted confectioners' sugar. Bake for just 4–5 minutes, until golden. Serve immediately.

teatime treats

raspberry shortcakes

Base:

1½ cups all-purpose flour

scant ¼ cup cornstarch

a pinch of salt

⅓ cup superfine or granulated
    sugar

10 tablespoons unsalted butter,
    straight from the fridge, diced,
    plus extra for the pan

Filling:

½ cup fresh raspberries

½ cup good raspberry jam

Topping:

½ cup porridge oats

3 tablespoons light brown
    muscovado sugar

a 7-inch square cake pan, greased

makes 9 shortcakes

These buttery shortcakes topped with fresh raspberries are ready in just 30 minutes. Keep some raspberries in the freezer so that you can make the shortcakes year round.

Preheat the oven to 350°F. Tip the flour, cornstarch, salt, and sugar into the bowl of a food processor. Pulse for a few seconds to mix the ingredients. Add the butter and work the processor until the mixture looks like fine crumbs.

Set aside one-third of the mixture for the topping. Tip the rest of the mixture into the prepared pan, making sure it is evenly spread. Bake in the preheated oven for 10 minutes then let cool while you make the filling and topping. Leave the oven on.

Put the raspberries and jam into a bowl and mix gently. Put to one side. Put the shortcake crumbs that you put aside into another mixing bowl with the oats and sugar. Squeeze the mixture together with your hands so it comes together into flakes. Spread the raspberry mixture over the baked shortcake then scatter with the oat topping. Bake in the oven for another 15–20 minutes, until golden. Let cool on a wire rack.

Cut the shortcake into 9 squares. Store in an airtight container and eat within 4 days.

oaty chocolate crunchies

3½ oz. semisweet chocolate
 (at least 70 percent cocoa solids),
 roughly chopped
1½ cups granola
12 paper cupcake liners

makes 12

A little chocolate now and again is fine—all the more so when it's high in iron-rich cocoa solids and melted over nutritious nuts, seeds, and oats.

Melt the chocolate in a heatproof bowl set over a saucepan of gently simmering, not boiling, water. Stir it occasionally, until smooth. Remove the bowl from the pan.

Add the granola to the chocolate and mix thoroughly. Put about 1 tablespoon of the mixture into each case. Leave for 1 hour until set before serving. Store in an airtight container for up to 1 week.

apricot & walnut bars

7 tablespoons sunflower margarine
2 tablespoons light brown sugar
5 tablespoons corn syrup
1¼ cups old-fashioned rolled oats
⅓ cup dried apricots, chopped
⅓ cup walnuts, chopped
a baking pan, 8 inches square,
 lightly greased

makes about 12

These oat bars are low in fat and packed with fiber, protein, and omega-3 fatty acids.

Preheat the oven to 350°F. Put the margarine, sugar, and syrup in a pan and heat gently, stirring occasionally, until the margarine has melted and the sugar has dissolved.

Remove the pan from the heat and add the oats, apricots, and walnuts. Stir well until thoroughly mixed, then press into the prepared baking pan with the back of a spoon.

Bake for 20–25 minutes until golden and firm. Let cool before cutting into bars. Leave until completely cold before removing from the pan. Store in an airtight container for up to 5 days.

oaty chocolate crunchies

sticky cinnamon buns

Pastry dough:

4 cups unbleached white bread flour

1 envelope or 2½ teaspoons
   active dry yeast

1 teaspoon salt

3 tablespoons superfine or
   granulated sugar

1 extra-large egg,
   at room temperature

1⅓ cups milk, lukewarm

3 tablespoons unsalted butter,
   very soft

Filling:

2 tablespoons butter, very soft

1 teaspoon ground cinnamon

4 tablespoons soft light brown sugar

½ cup pecan pieces or raisins

a baking sheet, very well greased

makes 12 buns

These buns smell as good as they taste. The recipe yields twelve buns and you'll be hard pressed to keep the children's hands off them.

Put the dry dough ingredients in a bowl and mix. Make a well in the center. Add the egg, milk, and butter in the center. Use your hands to slowly stir the flour into the liquid in the center, until it has all been mixed in. If the dough feels dry, add a little more milk. If it feels sticky, add a little flour. Gather into a ball and knead for 5 minutes on a floured work surface. Leave the dough covered in a warm place until it has doubled—about 1 hour.

Uncover the bowl and gently punch down the dough. Roll it out on a lightly floured work surface, to make a rectangle about 10 x 14 inches. Spread the butter for the filling over the dough. Mix the cinnamon and sugar and sprinkle over the butter. Lastly, scatter the nuts or raisins over the dough and lightly press down.

Roll up the dough from one of the long sides to make a roll, then pinch the 'seam' of the dough to seal it. Cut into 12 pieces. Put the rolls on the baking sheet, cut side up so the spiral filling is exposed. Cover the sheet with a dry tea towel and leave to rise for 20 minutes. Preheat the oven to 425°F. Bake the buns for 20 minutes, until golden brown. Eat warm or at room temperature. They will keep for 2 days in a container.

gingerbread teddy bears

1 stick butter

2 tablespoons corn syrup

2⅓ cups all-purpose flour

1 teaspoon baking soda

1 teaspoon ground ginger

¾ cup soft brown sugar

1 egg, beaten

icing tubes in assorted colors and
    dragées, to decorate

*teddy-bear-shaped cookie cutters in
    assorted sizes*

2 baking sheets, greased

makes about 10 bears

Look out for teddy-bear-shaped cookie cutters in kitchen shops. Ready-made colored icing sold in squeezy tubes makes it easier for small children to help with the decorating.

Warm the butter and syrup in a saucepan until melted, then set aside to cool. Combine the flour, baking soda, ginger, and sugar in a bowl. Make a well in the center. Pour in the butter and syrup, add the egg, then mix well to combine. Knead lightly to form a soft dough, then wrap it in plastic wrap and refrigerate for about 20 minutes.

Preheat the oven to 375°F.

Roll out the dough on a lightly floured work surface and stamp out the teddy bear shapes using cookie cutters. Transfer the shapes to the baking sheets and bake in the preheated oven for 7–8 minutes, until starting to color around the edges. Let cool on the sheets for about 3 minutes, then transfer to a wire rack to cool completely. Decorate the bears as you wish.

peach & almond tartlets

3/4 cup plus 2 tablespoons
    whole-wheat flour

1/3 cup ground almonds

a pinch of salt

2 1/2 tablespoons sugar

6 tablespoons polyunsaturated
    margarine

1 egg, beaten

plain yogurt, to serve

cubes of fresh peach, to serve

pure maple syrup or honey,
    to serve

a tartlet pan, well greased

makes 8–10 tartlets

Children will love this recipe. Almonds have the highest protein content of any nut as well as being rich in magnesium, potassium, and phosphorous, and especially rich in calcium. They are also high in monounsaturated fat so really, these tartlets are positively good for you!

Preheat the oven to 375°F.

Mix the flour, almonds, salt, and sugar together in a bowl and rub in the margarine. Mix in the egg to form a soft dough.

Roll out the dough thinly on a lightly floured surface. Cut into 8–10 circles to fit your tartlet pan. Arrange in the pan and bake in the preheated oven for 15 minutes. Let cool.

Fill each tartlet with a dollop of yogurt, then top with the peaches and drizzle with maple syrup.

Store any remaining tartlet cases in an airtight container for up to 2 days, or freeze in batches of 4–6 and warm up in the oven. Try other fillings, such as sliced strawberries mixed with a little lemon juice and served with a spoonful of whipped cream.

white chocolate
& raspberry tartlets

10 oz. puff pastry dough,
    thawed if frozen

3½ oz. white chocolate, roughly
    chopped

2 eggs

6 tablespoons heavy cream,

¼ cup sugar

10 oz. raspberries

all-purpose flour, to sprinkle

confectioners' sugar, to dust

a 12-hole muffin pan

*a cookie cutter roughly the same size as
    the muffin pan holes*

makes 12 tartlets

These little tarts look so elegant and taste great, yet they're very easy to make. They will fly off the plates, straight into your children's sticky fingers.

Preheat the oven to 350°F.

Turn the dough out onto a lightly floured surface. Using a rolling pin, roll it out until it is about ⅛-inch thick. Cut the dough into rounds using the cookie cutter and press them gently into the muffin pan holes.

Melt the chocolate in a heatproof bowl set over a saucepan of gently simmering water, making sure that the bottom of the bowl does not touch the water. Stir the chocolate with a wooden spoon until it has melted. Take it off the heat and let cool.

Beat the eggs in a large bowl with a wire whisk until smooth. Whisk in the cream and sugar followed by the melted chocolate, making sure the mixture is nice and smooth.

Carefully fill the tartlet crusts with the mixture using a small spoon. Bake in the preheated oven for about 15 minutes, until the pastry has puffed up and is golden in color. Let cool. Put 3 or 4 raspberries on top of each crust, dust with sifted confectioners' sugar, and serve.

do-it-yourself party cupcakes

1 stick unsalted butter,
    at room temperature
½ cup granulated sugar
2 eggs
1 cup self-rising flour
1½ tablespoons unsweetened
    cocoa powder

To decorate:
1½ sticks unsalted butter,
    at room temperature
3 cups confectioners' sugar, sifted
2 tablespoons milk
lilac, yellow, and green food coloring
brightly colored candies, such as
    Jimmies, Smarties, Skittles, Dots,
    and gumdrops
sprinkles, sugar flowers, and edible
    colored balls
a 12-hole cupcake pan, lined with
    paper liners

makes 12 cupcakes

These decorate-your-own-cakes are always a hit at kids' parties. Everyone will love getting creative and trying to produce the most outlandish cupcake at the table. Just be sure to make plenty of frosting and search out pretty decorations.

Preheat the oven to 350°F.

Beat the butter and sugar in a bowl until pale and fluffy, then beat in the eggs, one at a time. Sift the flour and cocoa powder into the mixture and fold in. Spoon the mixture into the paper liners and bake in the preheated oven for about 17 minutes until risen and a skewer inserted in the center comes out clean. Transfer to a wire rack to cool completely.

To decorate, beat the butter until soft, then add the sugar and milk and beat until smooth and creamy. Divide the frosting among three bowls. Add a few drops of food coloring to each one and stir well to make a vibrant lilac, yellow, and green topping. Spoon into serving bowls.

Arrange the cakes on a plate and put the decorations in individual bowls alongside the bowls of frosting. Let the kids decorate their own cupcakes.

ice cream cupcakes

4 tablespoons unsalted butter,
  at room temperature
¼ cup granulated sugar
1 egg, beaten
generous ⅓ cup self-rising flour

To decorate:
2 oz. bittersweet chocolate,
  roughly chopped
2½ tablespoons heavy cream
1 tablespoon corn syrup
ice cream
*a 12-hole cupcake pan, lined with
  paper liners*

makes 12 cupcakes

These cupcakes are perfect for serving at a party but they can be messy so be sure to have plenty of napkins at the ready for wiping sticky fingers! Choose any flavor of ice cream you like.

Preheat the oven to 350°F.

Beat the butter and sugar in a mixing bowl until pale and fluffy, then gradually beat in the egg. Sift the flour into the mix and fold in. Spoon the mixture into the paper liners and bake in the preheated oven for about 15 minutes until risen and golden and a skewer inserted in the center comes out clean. Transfer to a wire rack and let cool. Use a serrated knife to cut a shallow hole out of the center of the cupcakes. Keep what you've cut out for lids.

To decorate, put the chocolate, cream, and syrup in a small saucepan and warm gently, stirring, until the chocolate starts to melt. Remove the pan from the heat and continue stirring until smooth and creamy and the chocolate has melted completely.

Using a melon baller, make small scoops of ice cream and place on top of the cupcakes. Replace the lids of the cakes, then spoon over the chocolate sauce and serve immediately.

chocolate brownie birthday cupcakes

3½ oz. bittersweet chocolate,
    roughly chopped
5 tablespoons unsalted butter
1 egg
⅓ cup granulated sugar
3 tablespoons self-rising flour
⅓ cup shelled macadamia nuts,
    pecans, or walnuts,
    coarsely chopped
2 mini-cupcake pans, lined with petits
    fours liners
12 mini-candles

makes 18 cupcakes

These gooey, chocolatey, nutty baby brownie cakes make a mouthwatering change from the traditional children's birthday cake. Choose any nuts you like—macadamia nuts add a lovely buttery taste. Put the cupcakes on a cake stand or plate and gently press a candle into each one. Turn out the lights, light the candles, and voilà!

Preheat the oven to 350°F.

Put the chocolate and butter in a heatproof bowl set over a pan of gently simmering water. Do not let the bowl touch the water. Stir until almost melted. Remove from the heat and let cool for about 5 minutes.

Beat in the egg, then stir in the sugar. Sift the flour into the mixture and fold in, then stir in the nuts.

Spoon the mixture into the petits fours liners and bake in the preheated oven for about 17 minutes until the top has turned pale and crackly and is just firm to the touch. Let cool on a wire rack, before serving with a glowing candle in the center of each cupcake.

fresh fruit torte

Base:

1½ cups all-purpose flour

1 teaspoon baking powder

½ teaspoon ground cinnamon

¼ cup superfine or granulated sugar

yolks from 2 extra-large eggs

½ stick unsalted butter, chilled
   and diced

10 oz. fresh blueberries, blackberries,
   or cherries (pitted), OR 14 oz.
   apricots or plums, pitted

Topping:

¼ cup all-purpose flour

¼ teaspoon ground cinnamon

2 tablespoons superfine or
   granulated sugar

2 tablespoons ground almonds

2 tablespoons unsalted butter,
   chilled and diced

*a springform cake pan about 8 inches
   in diameter, greased and lined with
   baking parchment*

makes 1 large torte

Children will almost always favor chocolate over fruit for dessert but this wonderfully rich torte is sure to win them over. Serve with some yogurt.

Preheat the oven to 350°F.

Put the flour, baking powder, cinnamon, and sugar into the bowl of a food processor. Pulse to mix the ingredients together. Add the egg yolks and butter to the processor. Pulse to mix all the ingredients until they look like very large crumbs.

Tip the crumbs into the cake pan and spread evenly. Press the mixture firmly into the pan with the back of a spoon to make an even layer. Scatter the blueberries, blackberries, or cherries over the cake mixture. If using apricots or plums cut in half, cut each into 8 slices. Arrange the fruit over the base.

Put all the ingredients for the topping into the bowl of the food processor. Process until they look like big bread crumbs. You can also do this in a bowl using your fingers.

Scatter the topping evenly over the fruit. Put the cake pan on a baking sheet then bake for 35 minutes, until golden. Remove from the oven and let cool on a wire rack until warm, then unclip the pan and remove the torte. Dust with sifted confectioners' sugar before serving either warm or at room temperature.

toffee loaf cake

2 cups all-purpose flour

1 teaspoon baking soda

1 cup firmly packed brown sugar

½ cup plain yogurt

½ cup milk

1 extra-large egg

1½ tablespoons unsalted butter, melted

½ cup chopped pecans, mixed nuts, or raisins

a loaf pan (8½ x 4½ x 2½ inches) greased and lined with parchment paper

makes 1 medium cake

This loaf cake is perfect for picnics and lunchboxes, and you can add the children's favorite nuts or dried fruit to the recipe.

Preheat the oven to 350°F.

Put the flour, baking soda, and sugar in a bowl.

Pour the yogurt into a measuring cup, then top up with the milk to make 1 cup. Break the egg into the cup, add the butter, then mix the ingredients with a fork.

Pour the liquids in the cup into the bowl. Mix well with a wooden spoon for 1 minute, then mix in the nuts or fruit. Spoon into the pan. Bake in the preheated oven for about 45–50 minutes until golden brown. Insert a skewer into the center of the cake—if it comes out clean, then the cake is cooked; if it is coated in cake mix, then cook for about 5 minutes more.

Put the pan on a wire rack to cool. Leave for 10 minutes, then lift the loaf out of the pan using the parchment paper. Let cool on the wire rack. Serve in thick slices. The loaf will keep for up to 4 days in an airtight container or freeze it for up to 1 month.

apple tea bread

1⅓ cups whole-wheat self-rising flour
½ cup light brown sugar
2 teaspoons baking powder, sifted
½ teaspoon baking soda
1 teaspoon ground cinnamon
½ teaspoon freshly grated nutmeg
1 large apple, cored and grated
⅓ cup raisins
⅓ cup walnuts, chopped
7 tablespoons unsalted butter, melted
1 egg, beaten
about ⅓ cup apple juice
*a loaf pan, 9 x 3 inches, lightly greased
and lined with parchment paper*

makes 1 loaf

This tea bread is so versatile. It's great eaten just as it is for picnics, but it's also delicious served as a quick snack with some Cheddar cheese and grapes on top. Alternatively, serve it warm topped with a little yogurt.

Preheat the oven to 350°F.

Put the flour, sugar, baking powder, and spices in a large bowl and mix. Stir in the grated apple, raisins, and walnuts. Mix well.

Mix in the melted butter, then stir in the beaten egg and the apple juice to give a soft dropping consistency. Add a little more apple juice if the mixture is too stiff.

Spoon the mixture into the prepared pan and bake in the preheated oven for 45–50 minutes until cooked. To check, insert a skewer into the center of the loaf; it should come out clean. Remove from the oven and let cool in the pan. Serve in slices. Store in an airtight container for up to 5 days, or wrap and freeze for up to 1 month.

fresh orange cake

1 unwaxed orange, washed and halved

1½ sticks unsalted butter, very soft, plus extra for greasing the pan

1¼ cups superfine or granulated sugar

3 extra-large eggs, at room temperature

2 cups all-purpose flour

1 teaspoon baking soda

½ cup milk

3 tablespoons plain yogurt

3 tablespoons superfine or granulated sugar, for the topping

a large loaf pan, greased and lined with baking parchment

makes 1 large loaf cake

This all-in-one loaf cake is easy to make so get the children involved. The fresh orange gives it a wonderfully fresh flavor.

Preheat the oven to 350°F.

Remove the pips from one half of the orange, cut it into 8 pieces, skin still on, and blend in a food processor until finely chopped. Transfer to a bowl or the bowl of an electric mixer. Add the butter, sugar, and eggs then sift in the flour and baking soda. Next, add the milk and yogurt then beat with a spoon or electric mixer (on low speed) for 1 minute until well mixed and there are no streaks of flour. Spoon the mixture into the prepared pan.

Bake for about 50 minutes, until golden. Insert a skewer in the center of the cake—if it comes out clean, then the loaf is ready. If it is sticky with mixture, then cook the loaf for another 5 minutes.

To make the topping, squeeze the juice of the other orange half into a bowl then stir in the sugar to make a thick, syrupy glaze.

Leave the loaf pan to stand on a wire rack. Prick the top of the loaf all over with a toothpick and spoon over the syrup. Let cool completely before removing from the pan. Cut the cake into thick slices. Store in an airtight container and eat it within 4 days.

sticky gingerbread

2 sticks unsalted butter

1 cup dark brown sugar

$^2/_3$ cup black treacle or molasses

2 eggs, beaten

$2^1/_3$ cups all-purpose flour

2 teaspoons ground cinnamon

1 tablespoon ground ginger

1 teaspoon baking soda

$1^1/_4$ cups warm milk

*2 x 2-lb loaf pans, greased and
  lined with baking parchment*

makes 2 large loaves

This classic teatime recipe yields two loaves—you can bake them both together then pop one in the freezer to eat a week later. Alternatively, if you have a lot of mouths to feed, this cake mix can be baked in one 10-inch round cake pan, but it will need to cook for 1½ hours.

Preheat the oven to 275°F.

Put the butter, sugar, and treacle in a large saucepan and heat gently, stirring constantly until melted.

Remove from the heat, let cool slightly, and stir in the eggs. Sift the flour, cinnamon, and ginger into the melted mixture.

Mix together the baking soda and warm milk. Add to the ginger mixture, mix well, and pour equal amounts of the cake mixture into each pan.

Bake in the preheated oven for just under 1 hour. The top of the cake will be slightly golden with a lovely crust and a skewer should come out clean.

chocolate fudge birthday cake

3½ oz. bittersweet chocolate,
    roughly chopped

3 tablespoons unsweetened cocoa

⅓ cup water, very hot but not boiling

1½ sticks unsalted butter, softened

1¼ cups superfine or granulated sugar

3 extra-large eggs

1 cup plain yogurt

2 cups all-purpose flour

2 teaspoons baking powder

1 teaspoon baking soda

Chocolate frosting:

½ cup heavy cream

2 oz. milk chocolate,
    roughly chopped

2 oz. bittersweet chocolate,
    roughly chopped

your choice of decorations

*a springform cake pan, 9 inches
    diameter, greased and lined with
    baking parchment*

serves 8–10

This delicious, chocolatey cake is perfect for birthdays. It tastes best made a day ahead.

Preheat the oven to 325°F. Put the chocolate, cocoa powder, and hot water in a heatproof mixing bowl. Leave for 1 minute then stir until the mix is smooth and melted.

Put the butter and sugar into a bowl. Beat well, then gradually add the eggs and beat until very smooth. Pour in the melted chocolate mixture and mix well. Spoon in the yogurt, sift in the flour, baking powder, and baking soda and mix well. Spoon into the prepared pan, then spread evenly so it is smooth.

Bake for 55 minutes. Insert a skewer in the center of the cake— if it comes out clean, then the cake is ready. If not, bake for another 5 minutes. Remove from the oven and set the pan on a wire rack. Let cool for 5 minutes then unclip the pan and let the cake cool completely. Don't worry if it sinks a bit.

To make the frosting, heat the cream in a saucepan until it is scalding hot, but not quite boiling. Take off the heat. Put the two kinds of chocolate in a heatproof bowl and pour over the hot cream. Leave for 2 minutes then stir until smooth. Let cool.

Put the cake upside down on a plate. Spread the frosting on the top and sides of the cake to cover it completely. Decorate with sprinkles and sweets. Let cool until firm before serving.

scones

2 cups all-purpose flour
4 teaspoons baking powder
a good pinch of salt
1/4 cup superfine or granulated sugar
4 tablespoons unsalted butter, at
  room temperature, diced, plus a
  little extra for greasing
1 extra-large egg, lightly beaten
about 1/2 cup milk
a baking sheet, greased
a cookie cutter, about 2½ inches
  in diameter

makes about 8 scones

Scones are quick and easy to make so get the
children involved. Add raisins if you like, or omit
the sugar and add some grated cheese.

Preheat the oven to 425°F.

Sift the flour, baking powder, salt, and sugar into a bowl. Rub the
butter into the flour with your fingertips until the mixture looks
like crumbs. Make a well in the center.

Put the egg into a measuring cup along with enough milk to make
2/3 cup in total. Pour three-quarters of the milk mixture into the
center. Using a knife, combine the liquid and flour mix to make
a soft, coarse-looking dough. If the dough is dry and crumbly stir
in more of the milk mixture a tablespoon at a time.

Work and knead the ball of dough on a lightly floured work
surface for a few seconds so it looks smoother. Flatten the dough
until it is about 1¼ inches thick. Dip the cutter in flour then cut
out rounds. Gather up the scraps into a ball to make more.

Put all the rounds onto the prepared baking sheet, setting them
slightly apart and bake in the preheated oven for 12–15 minutes,
until golden. Transfer the scones to a wire rack. They taste best
eaten the same day.

drinks

lemon cordial

freshly squeezed juice and
     grated zest of 6 unwaxed lemons
2 cups unrefined granulated sugar

To serve:
lemon slices
ice cubes (optional)

makes 2 quarts

Packed with vitamin C, this delicious drink is
sure to quench the children's thirst on a hot day.

Put the lemon juice in a large bowl, add the sugar, and stir well.

Put the lemon zest and 5 cups cold water in a saucepan and
bring to a boil. Reduce the heat and simmer for 3 minutes. Strain
through a fine mesh strainer onto the lemon juice and sugar
mixture and stir until the sugar has dissolved. Discard the zest.

Cover loosely and let cool completely. Dilute the cordial to taste
with cold water and add slices of lemon and ice cubes, if liked.
Store in the refrigerator for up to 2 weeks.

apple & carrot juice

3 carrots, chopped
2 eating apples, peeled, cored,
     and chopped
2 tablespoons crushed ice,
     to serve (optional)

serves 2

This juice is high in soluble fiber, which is
necessary for a healthy digestive system, and
is full of immune-boosting antioxidants.

Push the carrot and apple pieces through a juicer. Put
1 tablespoon crushed ice, if using, in each of 2 tall glasses, pour
the juice over the top, and serve.

blueberry & orange smoothie

freshly squeezed juice of 4 oranges
1 basket blueberries (about 8 oz.)
sugar (optional)

serves 1–2

All fruits contain vitamin C, but oranges contain more than others. Use them to extend fruits that don't have much juice themselves, such as blueberries, strawberries, or apricots.

Put the orange juice in a blender, add the blueberries, and blend until smooth. Add sugar to taste, if using.

berry, apricot, & orange slush

8 ripe apricots, halved and pitted,
    then coarsely chopped
8 strawberries, hulled and halved
freshly squeezed juice of 2 oranges

serves 1

This delightful slush is ready in just minutes and far cheaper to make at home with the children than to buy from the store.

Put the apricots, strawberries, and orange juice into a blender and purée until smooth, adding water if needed. (If the mixture is too thick, add ice cubes and blend again.)

fresh raspberry lemonade

2 large unwaxed lemons
1/3 cup sugar
6 oz. fresh or frozen raspberries,
    about 1 cup
2 cups sparkling mineral water
12 ice cubes

serves 4

This fizzy, refreshing, healthy cool drink really
is summer in a glass. It's sure to lure the kids
away from storebought carbonated drinks that
are laced with additives and sweeteners.

Cut each lemon into 8. Put the lemons, sugar, raspberries, and
1 cup cold water in a blender. Blend for 10 seconds. If there are
still large pieces of lemon left, blend again for 5 seconds. Remove
the blender pitcher from the machine.

Put a medium strainer on top of a large serving pitcher. Carefully
pour the lemon mixture into the pitcher through the strainer.
Using a spoon, gently press down on the lemons to squeeze out
all the juice. Throw away the lemon pieces.

Top up the juice with the sparkling water. Stir in the ice cubes and
serve in chilled glasses.

chocolate monkey milkshake

1¼ cup lowfat milk (use whole milk
   for children under 5)
¾ cup plain yogurt
2 ripe bananas, sliced
2 tablespoons crushed ice (optional)
2 teaspoons finely grated semisweet
   chocolate (at least 70 percent
   cocoa solids)

serves 2

Bananas are the perfect fast food. They are filling and high in potassium and vitamin B6—perfect for keeping your little monkeys satisfied.

Put the milk, yogurt, and bananas in a blender and process until smooth. Put 1 tablespoon crushed ice, if using, in each of 2 tall glasses and pour the milkshake over the top. Sprinkle with the grated chocolate and serve immediately.

honey, apple, & banana shake

2 ripe bananas, sliced
1 cup plain yogurt
2 teaspoons honey
¾ cup apple juice
ice cubes, to serve (optional)

serves 2

Try this fruitier twist on the shake above. The honey, apple, and banana flavors make a winning combination.

Put the bananas, yogurt, honey, and apple juice in a blender and process until smooth. Pour into 2 tall glasses, add ice cubes, if using, and serve immediately.

scones

2 cups all-purpose flour

4 teaspoons baking powder

a good pinch of salt

¼ cup superfine or granulated sugar

4 tablespoons unsalted butter, at
    room temperature, diced, plus a
    little extra for greasing

1 extra-large egg, lightly beaten

about ½ cup milk

a baking sheet, greased

*a cookie cutter, about 2½ inches
    in diameter*

makes about 8 scones

Scones are quick and easy to make so get the children involved. Add raisins if you like, or omit the sugar and add some grated cheese.

Preheat the oven to 425°F.

Sift the flour, baking powder, salt, and sugar into a bowl. Rub the butter into the flour with your fingertips until the mixture looks like crumbs. Make a well in the center.

Put the egg into a measuring cup along with enough milk to make ⅔ cup in total. Pour three-quarters of the milk mixture into the center. Using a knife, combine the liquid and flour mix to make a soft, coarse-looking dough. If the dough is dry and crumbly stir in more of the milk mixture a tablespoon at a time.

Work and knead the ball of dough on a lightly floured work surface for a few seconds so it looks smoother. Flatten the dough until it is about 1¼ inches thick. Dip the cutter in flour then cut out rounds. Gather up the scraps into a ball to make more.

Put all the rounds onto the prepared baking sheet, setting them slightly apart and bake in the preheated oven for 12–15 minutes, until golden. Transfer the scones to a wire rack. They taste best eaten the same day.

honey, apple & banana shake

mango smoothie

1 ripe mango, peeled and sliced
1 ripe banana, sliced
1 cup chilled fresh orange juice
ice cubes, to serve (optional)

serves 2

This smoothie is perfect on a really hot day when you want to give your children a filling drink, but would rather avoid a calorie-laden milkshake.

Put all the mango slices and any juice into a large blender or food processor, along with the banana slices. Pour in the orange juice. Blend the mixture until completely smooth and foamy. Pour into tall glasses and add ice cubes, if using.

strawberry milkshake

1 pint ripe strawberries, hulled
   and sliced
1 ripe banana, sliced
3/4 cup lowfat milk (use whole milk
   for children under 5)
ice cubes, to serve (optional)

serves 2

This is a simple fruit and milk recipe—but you can add a scoop of strawberry ice cream or sorbet if you want something a little more substantial.

Put the strawberries and banana into the blender, then add the cold milk. Blend the mixture until smooth and foaming. Pour into chilled glasses and add ice cubes, if using.

peach melba ripple

4 canned peach halves in natural
   juice, drained
1 teaspoon pure vanilla extract
2 cups lowfat milk (use whole milk
   for children under 5)
4 scoops vanilla ice cream
1 cup raspberries

serves 2–3

You can simply blend all the ingredients for this recipe together in one go, but the kids will love the rippled effect of swirling the peach and raspberry flavors together just before serving.

Put the peach halves, half the vanilla extract, half the milk, and 2 scoops of vanilla ice cream in a blender. Blend until smooth and divide between 2 or 3 tumblers. Repeat with the raspberries and remaining vanilla, milk, and ice cream. Drizzle the raspberry mixture carefully into the glasses to give a ripple effect.

lemon cheesecake shake

3½ oz. cream cheese
grated zest and freshly squeezed juice
   of ½ unwaxed lemon
¼ cup prepared lemon curd
½ cup Greek yogurt
1 cup lowfat milk (use whole milk
   for children under 5)

serves 3–4

Sharp and tangy, this rich drink is just like cheesecake in a glass. Serve it with graham crackers or ginger cookies, depending on what the kids prefer, and it's almost like the real thing!

Put all the ingredients in a blender and blend until smooth.

real hot chocolate

real hot chocolate

1½ oz. bittersweet chocolate,
    roughly chopped
1 teaspoon sugar
⅔ cup lowfat milk (use whole milk
    for children under 5)

To serve (optional):
whipped cream
mini-marshmallows

serves 1

The real thing—bittersweet chocolate, milk, and
a dash of sugar, plus whipped cream and mini-
marshmallows if you really want to have fun.

Put the chocolate, sugar, and milk in a small saucepan. Heat
until almost boiling. Stir occasionally with a wooden spoon to
help the chocolate melt.

Using a rotary beater, beat the mixture until it is very smooth and
foaming. Carefully pour the hot chocolate into a mug. Top with
a swirl of cream, sprinkle with marshmallows, then serve.

vanilla soyaccino

2 cups soy milk
1 teaspoon pure vanilla extract
4 teaspoons maple syrup
ground cinnamon or cocoa powder,
    to serve

serves 2

For children who are lactose intolerant, soy milk
is a great way of enjoying other "milky" drinks.

Put the soy milk, vanilla extract, and maple syrup in a saucepan
and gently heat until it just reaches boiling point. Remove from
the heat and then froth the milk, using a milk frother or balloon
whisk. Pour it into 2 cups, dust with ground cinnamon or cocoa
powder and serve immediately.

babyccino

1 cup lowfat milk (use whole milk for
    children under 5)
2 teaspoons chocolate syrup or sauce
sweetened cocoa powder, to dust
mini-marshmallows, to serve
    (optional)

serves 2

It's always cute to see small children emulating their parents with a "minilatte"—of course these are made without coffee but they look great with the drizzle of chocolate syrup.

Put the milk in a saucepan and heat gently until warm, but not hot, then froth the milk using a frother or whisk. Drizzle a little chocolate syrup inside 2 glasses and add the milk. Dust with cocoa powder, top with marshmallows, if using, and serve.

chocolate milk with ice cream

2 tablespoons sweetened
    cocoa powder
2 cups lowfat milk (use whole milk
    for children under 5)
2 scoops vanilla ice cream
2 tablespoons chocolate syrup
    or sauce

serves 2

This is guaranteed to become a big favorite with the kids. You can top it with any flavor ice cream you like—chocolate or caramel work well.

Combine the cocoa powder with about 2 tablespoons of the milk and mix to form a smooth paste. Gently heat the remaining milk in a saucepan until it just reaches boiling point and whisk into the chocolate mixture until evenly blended.

Divide between 2 cups and top with a scoop of ice cream and some chocolate syrup. Serve immediately with spoons.

babyccino

index

conversion charts

Weights and measures have been rounded up or down slightly to make measuring easier.

Volume equivalents:

American	Metric	Imperial
1 teaspoon	5 ml	
1 tablespoon	15 ml	
¼ cup	60 ml	2 fl.oz.
⅓ cup	75 ml	2½ fl.oz.
½ cup	125 ml	4 fl.oz.
⅔ cup	150 ml	5 fl.oz. (¼ pint)
¾ cup	175 ml	6 fl.oz.
1 cup	250 ml	8 fl.oz.

1 stick butter = 8 tablespoons = 125 g

Weight equivalents:

Imperial	Metric
1 oz.	25 g
2 oz.	50 g
3 oz.	75 g
4 oz.	125 g
5 oz.	150 g
6 oz.	175 g
7 oz.	200 g
8 oz. (½ lb.)	250 g
9 oz.	275 g
10 oz.	300 g
11 oz.	325 g
12 oz.	375 g
13 oz.	400 g
14 oz.	425 g
15 oz.	475 g
16 oz. (1 lb.)	500 g
2 lb.	1 kg

Measurements:

Inches	Cm
¼ inch	5 mm
½ inch	1 cm
¾ inch	1.5 cm
1 inch	2.5 cm
2 inches	5 cm
3 inches	7 cm
4 inches	10 cm
5 inches	12 cm
6 inches	15 cm
7 inches	18 cm
8 inches	20 cm
9 inches	23 cm
10 inches	25 cm
11 inches	28 cm
12 inches	30 cm

Oven temperatures:

110°C	(225°F)	Gas ¼
120°C	(250°F)	Gas ½
140°C	(275°F)	Gas 1
150°C	(300°F)	Gas 2
160°C	(325°F)	Gas 3
180°C	(350°F)	Gas 4
190°C	(375°F)	Gas 5
200°C	(400°F)	Gas 6
220°C	(425°F)	Gas 7
230°C	(450°F)	Gas 8
240°C	(475°F)	Gas 9

recipe credits

SUSANNAH BLAKE
Chocolate brownie birthday cupcakes
Do-it-yourself cupcakes
Gingerbread teddy bears
Ice cream cupcakes

TAMSIN BURNETT-HALL
Cornbread muffins
Goan shrimp curry
Niçoise tuna lunchbox
Tarragon chicken casserole

LINDA COLLISTER
American pancakes with blueberries
Baked Alaska
Brownies & ice cream
Chocolate fudge birthday cake
Chorizo & cheese muffins
Cornish bread
Freeform peach pie
Fresh fruit torte
Fresh orange cake
Fresh raspberry lemonade
Lamb koftas with pita pockets
Mango smoothie
Oven-fried chicken nuggets with potato wedges
Raspberry shortcake
Real hot chocolate
Scones
Sticky cinnamon buns
Strawberry milkshake
Sweet & spicy soup
Toffee loaf cake
Tuna pasta salad

Vegetable mini-frittatas
Zingy pasta

ROSS DOBSON
Baked lemon pudding

SILVANA FRANCO
Charred vegetable pizza
Fiorentina pizzas
Pancetta & chicken meatballs
Parsley & pancetta cannelloni

LIZ FRANKLIN
Creamy pea soup
Leek frittata
Pasta butterflies with zucchini, raisins, & pine nuts
Salmon skewers
Summer fruit tart
Sweet polenta pudding
Upside-down cheese & tomato tart
White chocolate & raspberry tartlets

TONIA GEORGE
Pappardelle with breaded chicken

NICOLA GRAIMES
Carrot & walnut muffins

AMANDA GRANT
Apricot slices
Cereal bars
Chicken & bell pepper stew
Coleslaw
Creamy potato salad
Falafel in pita
Fresh fruit jello

Lemon shortbread with berries
Meaty sandwiches
Potato, pesto, & tuna salad
Puff pinwheels
Sausage & chutney sandwich
Sausage & red pepper rolls
Sesame sausages
Smoked mackerel pâté
Spinach & onion tortilla
Sticky gingerbread

RACHAEL ANNE HILL
Apple & carrot juice
Apple & oat muffins
Apple tea bread
Apricot & walnut bars
Beef bourguignon
Berry berry peachy purée
Buttermilk drop scones with bananas & maple syrup
Carrot & hummus pitas
Cheese straws
Chicken & avocado rolls
Chili con carne
Chocolate monkey milkshake
Date & seed bars
Easy ratatouille & couscous
Fish cakes
Fish pie
Frozen fruit pops
Guacamole
Herby trout triangles
Honey, apple, & banana shake
Hummus

Ice cream sundaes
Lemon cordial
Little cherub's cherry semolina
Mini-meatballs & couscous with five-veg sauce
Mozzarella-topped herby veg loaf
Muesli
Nut burgers
Oatmeal pots with warm strawberry sauce
Oaty chocolate crunchies
Pan-fried mini beef patties with sautéed collard greens
Peach & almond tartlets
Pink porridge
Pumpkin soup
Roasted root dippers
Simple vegetable quiche
Smoked salmon bagels
Smoked trout & farfalle pasta
Sticky toffee & apricot sauce
Super-healthy blueberry mini-muffins
Whole-wheat breadsticks with avocado & tomato dip

ELSA PETERSEN-SCHEPELERN
Alphabet soup
Berry, apricot, & orange slush
Blueberry & orange smoothie

LOUISE PICKFORD
Babyccino

Chocolate milk with ice cream
Lemon cheesecake shake
Peach melba ripple
Vanilla soyaccino

FRAN WARDE
Almond fruit crumble
Banana, pecan, & granola yogurt pot
Chorizo & bean triangles
Eggs cocotte
Frozen berry yogurt cup
Lemon polenta cake
Minestrone with

pesto
Omelet
Oven-roasted vegetables with chickpeas & couscous
Pasta with ham & peas
Poached eggs
Scrambled eggs
Seasonal fruit tray tart
Tomato, basil, & mozzarella pizza
Whole-wheat banana & chocolate muffins

photography credits

Key: a=above, b=below, r=right, l=left, c=center.

CAROLINE ARBER
pages 1, 5, 8r, 10, 17, 18, 21, 36, 79, 86, 98, 117, 167, 172, 176

MARTIN BRIGDALE
pages 193, 198, 201, 202

PETER CASSIDY
page 43

VANESSA DAVIES
pages 9, 29, 33, 34r, 44, 58c, 83, 101, 154c, 180, 206, 218c, 218r, 224, 228, 232

TARA FISHER
pages 2, 3cl, 3cr, 6, 30, 34l, 47, 48, 51, 52, 58l, 60, 67, 68, 71, 76, 80, 85, 89, 90, 93, 94, 96 all, 97, 105, 123, 127, 132, 139, 143, 147, 150, 156, 159, 160, 184r, 194, 212

RICHARD JUNG
page 175

LISA LINDER
pages 34c, 40, 59, 75, 102, 124, 153, 154l, 171, 179, 197

WILLIAM LINGWOOD
pages 109, 110, 118, 121, 218l, 223, 235

NOEL MURPHY
pages 4, 8l, 13, 14, 25, 26, 39, 58r, 63, 64, 114, 131, 136, 144, 154r, 163, 164, 184l, 189, 209, 220, 227

WILLIAM REAVELL
pages 3l, 8c, 22, 56, 106, 113, 140, 149

IAN WALLACE
pages 219, 231

POLLY WREFORD
pages 3r, 35, 55, 72, 128, 135, 155, 168, 183, 184c, 185, 186, 190, 205, 211, 215, 216